SCROLL SAW
SCANDINAVIAN

Patterns & Projects

D1613666

SCROLL SAW
SCANDINAVIAN

Patterns & Projects

Patrick Spielman & Gösta Dahlqvist

Sterling Publishing Co., Inc.   New York

Library of Congress Cataloging-in-Publication Data

Spielman, Patrick E.
    Scroll saw Scandinavian patterns & projects / Patrick Spielman &
Gösta Dahlqvist.
        p.   cm.
    Includes index.
    ISBN 0-8069-0986-2
    1. Jig saws. 2. Woodwork—Patterns. 3. Woodwork—Scandinavia-
-Themes, motives. I. Dahlqvist, Gösta. II. Title. III. Title:
Scroll saw Scandinavian patterns and projects.
TT186.S67416   1995
745.51—dc20
                                                            94-47990
                                                            CIP

10 9 8 7 6 5 4 3 2

Published by Sterling Publishing Company, Inc.
387 Park Avenue South, New York, N.Y. 10016
© 1995 by Patrick Spielman and Gösta Dahlqvist
Distributed in Canada by Sterling Publishing
c/o Canadian Manda Group, One Atlantic Avenue, Suite 105
Toronto, Ontario, Canada M6K 3E7
Distributed in Great Britain and Europe by Cassell PLC
Wellington House, 125 Strand, London WC2R 0BB, England
Distributed in Australia by Capricorn Link (Australia) Pty Ltd.
P.O. Box 6651, Baulkham Hills, Business Centre, NSW 2153, Australia
Manufactured in the United States of America
All rights reserved

Sterling ISBN 0-8069-0986-2

Contents

Acknowledgments

Sincerest thanks and appreciation to our families for their help and wonderful cooperation. Special thanks to son Tommy Dahlqvist and his family, nephew Jan-Ake Dahlqvist, and friend Georg von Boisman for their valuable advice and assistance with translations.

The excellent drawings in this book are the work of our good friend and scroll-sawing associate Dirk Boelman, of The Art Factory. He has used his artistic skill to continually set new standards of excellence in the publication of scroll-saw patterns.

Thanks are also extended to graphic artists Sherri Valitchka and Barb Oleson Baryenbruch for their final shading touches and their helpful additions to the text. And we can't forget the help of our typist and scroll-sawing professional, Julie Kiehnau, for her prompt and talented efforts.

Metric Equivalents

INCHES TO MILLIMETRES AND CENTIMETRES

MM—millimetres   CM—centimetres

Inches	MM	CM	Inches	CM	Inches	CM
1/8	3	0.3	9	22.9	30	76.2
1/4	6	0.6	10	25.4	31	78.7
3/8	10	1.0	11	27.9	32	81.3
1/2	13	1.3	12	30.5	33	83.8
5/8	16	1.6	13	33.0	34	86.4
3/4	19	1.9	14	35.6	35	88.9
7/8	22	2.2	15	38.1	36	91.4
1	25	2.5	16	40.6	37	94.0
1 1/4	32	3.2	17	43.2	38	96.5
1 1/2	38	3.8	18	45.7	39	99.1
1 3/4	44	4.4	19	48.3	40	101.6
2	51	5.1	20	50.8	41	104.1
2 1/2	64	6.4	21	53.3	42	106.7
3	76	7.6	22	55.9	43	109.2
3 1/2	89	8.9	23	58.4	44	111.8
4	102	10.2	24	61.0	45	114.3
4 1/2	114	11.4	25	63.5	46	116.8
5	127	12.7	26	66.0	47	119.4
6	152	15.2	27	68.6	48	121.9
7	178	17.8	28	71.1	49	124.5
8	203	20.3	29	73.7	50	127.0

Introduction

This book features an interesting and generous variety of useful and well-designed scroll-saw projects with a Scandinavian theme. All are certain to appeal to men and women scroll sawyers of all ages. Some of the more ornate fretwork patterns were adapted from turn-of-the-century Swedish publications such as the *Allers Familie Journal*. Other patterns are original, simple contemporary designs that can be used to create functional pieces. This blend of old and new designs when combined with the capabilities of the modern scroll saw offers many possibilities. In fact, most of these patterns can be used to create three-dimensional, usable projects rather than just the typical flat cutouts.

This book offers more actual scroll-saw project patterns than were ever published in one volume. In order to provide as many patterns as we could, we had to present some patterns in one-half of their recommended size. However, with today's modern copy machines they can be enlarged easily and quickly, ready for sawing in just a few minutes.

These projects incorporate some new techniques seldom found in other scroll-saw project designs. They are: 1. the optional surface-carving (Illus. I-1) or wood-burning of line details that is easy to effect and that makes the finished project much more interesting and beautiful; and 2. extensive use of slot (mortise) and tab parts (Illus. I-2) in

Illus. I-1. This solid-wood key rack has been surface-carved.

Illus. I-2. This wheelbarrow project incorporates a number of slot (mortise)-and-tab joinery cuts.

Illus. I-3. The halved joints in this decorative holder for a warming candle allow the bottom of it to be easily assembled.

assembly or halved joints (Illus. I-3), in which the mating pieces slide into matching slots cut to the same width as the thickness of material being used (Illus. I-4). These unusual features allow you to make projects more artistically unique than those made with the typical contemporary scroll-saw patterns offered today. When the slot and tab assembly techniques are used, nails and screws are seldom required.

For those in the business of selling scroll-saw products, these designs are sure to be very popular. The easy assembly of the projects allows you to transport them knocked-down or to ship them flat for easy customer assembly. And, speaking of business potential, Gösta shares his numerous patterns and techniques for producing an exclusive and unique line of original wooden bookmarks (Illus. I-5) from paper-thin plywood. This is a proven business venture so successful it could be a full-time occupation in itself.

We also have included a brief chapter of

Illus. I-4. A project combining tabs and slots with halved joints. The corners slide vertically into each other, and the top and bottom are held in place by a decorative tab-and-slot joint assembly.

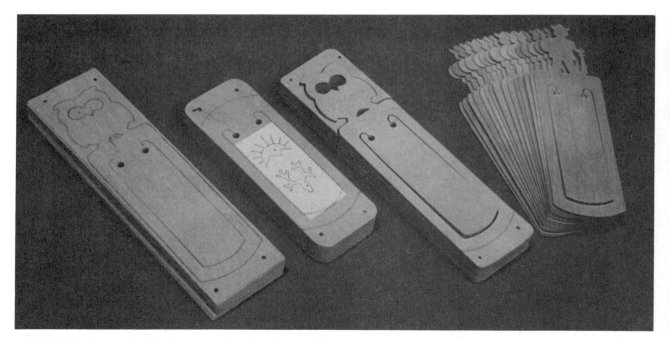

Illus. I-5. The essential elements involved in making Gösta's novel bookmarks. Multiple pieces are the result when you stack-saw these thin plywood bookmarks; this increases production and profitability.

helpful tips and suggestions intended to make it easier and more fun to create a scroll-saw project. In view of all that's offered in the following pages, we trust that this volume will be helpful and maybe profitable for you. However, most importantly, it is our intent to provide you with new, useful material that will expand your experiences with the scroll saw and make them more enjoyable.

Patrick Spielman
Gösta Dahlqvist
November 1994

Basic Tips

The patterns and projects in this book range from delightfully quick and simple to moderately challenging. All are fun and can be done with common tools and equipment found in typical home workshops. Most projects can be completed with just a scroll saw and drill to make the blade-entry holes for inside cutouts. A few projects may be done more easily and quickly with the aid of some other power saws, sanders, and routers. However, basic hand tools can also be utilized.

Youngsters and novice woodworkers should be supervised when they are working with power tools. Employ appropriate safety measures at all times for everyone inside the workshop. Always wear suitable eye, ear, and respiratory protection when any power tool is in use. For those new to scroll-sawing, we recommend *Scroll Saw Basics,* which covers all of the essential how-to techniques necessary to make the projects in this book.

Sizing Patterns with a Photocopier

To conserve space and to fit more projects into this book, it was necessary to print some of the patterns one-half of their original, recommended size. This information is noted on those particular patterns. These patterns must be enlarged. Usually they will be doubled in size, which is easily done with an office photocopy machine. To dou-

ble the size of a pattern, you must set the copy machine to 200 percent.

You may also elect to modify various patterns by enlarging (or reducing) them to any size. For example, the wheelbarrow projects on pages 60, 61, 72, 150, and 151 in enlarged versions make beautiful flower-holding projects for indoor decorating or exterior lawn ornaments.

Most communities have copy shops, but photocopiers with enlarging capabilities can also be found in public libraries and schools. Check the Yellow Pages of your telephone directory under the heading of Photocopying or Copying for the shop nearest you. New photocopiers are capable of enlarging any original pattern from this book to any size up to 200 percent, in one-percent increments. And you can get even greater enlargements by simply enlarging an already enlarged photocopy.

The cost of making a photocopy of a pattern from this book is minimal (usually just a few cents). Having a photocopy made is quick, convenient, and far more expedient and accurate than the other old-fashioned ways of copying or enlarging patterns that use the squared-grid system or pantograph tracings.

Enlarging Patterns with a Proportional Scale

A proportional scale (Illus. 1) is an inex-

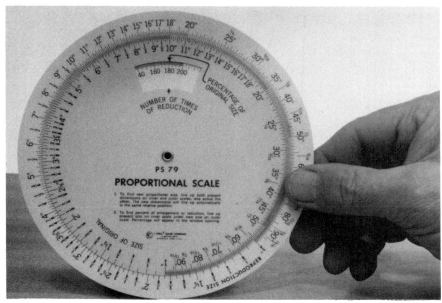

Illus. 1. A proportional scale makes precise enlargements or reductions of photocopied patterns quick and easy.

pensive device that can help you determine exactly what percentage of enlargement or reduction you will need to set the photocopier at to produce a pattern of a specific size. The scale is very easy to use; the little numbers and divisions make it look much more complicated than it really is. This device simply consists of two rotating discs, with numbers around their perimeters, joined by a common pivot. Align the dimension you have on the top disc with the dimension you want on the bottom disc. The exact percentage at which you will

need to set the copy machine will appear in the opening. This process eliminates guesswork and trial-and-error methods from the sizing process. It also saves you money spent on wasted photocopies. Proportional scales are found in art-, graphics-, and printing-supply stores. Check the Yellow Pages to locate a shop that sells these helpful devices.

To see how helpful this tool is, and how easy it actually is to use, follow the steps shown in Illus. 2–4.

Illus. 2. The problem: Enlarging this given pattern that's 3⁵⁄₁₆ inches long to a length of 6 inches.

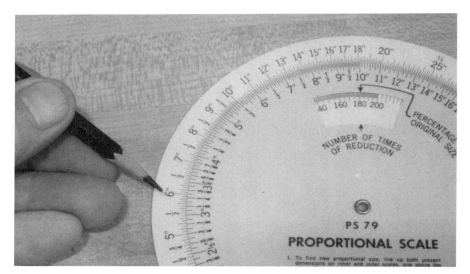

Illus. 3. Line up the 3⁵⁄₁₆-inch mark on the top disc with the 6-inch mark on the bottom disc. You must enlarge the pattern 180 percent, as given in the opening, to obtain one that's 6 inches in overall length.

Illus. 4. The enlarged 6-inch pattern is achieved in one step.

Wood Materials

Solid Woods. Exotic, highly figured woods are, as a rule, not required or recommended for the projects in this book. Such woods are expensive and not in the tradition of using basic, plain whitish woods. Pine, basswood, poplar, fir, and similar woods are good choices. They can be sawed and carved well and are fairly dimensionally stable woods that can also be painted. However, much Scandinavian woodwork is partially painted or left entirely unpainted and unfinished. Avoid cheaper wood grades that may have dark streaks or knots that would detract from the visual appeal of the wood.

Most of the projects require thin woods. If thin solid wood is not available locally or from your usual sources, contact West Friendship Hardwoods of West Friendship, Maryland; this company carries a variety of thinner solid woods milled exclusively for scroll-sawing.

Plywood. The majority of the projects are best sawn from plywood, especially those projects having delicate, thin, and fretted designs or those that are assembled with halved joints. Look for good plywood, that is, material with no voids in its interior plies and with two good faces. Various species in either metric or fractional thicknesses are available.

Plywood as thin as ¹⁄₆₄ inch is available, but most projects in this book utilize stock from ¹⁄₃₂ inch for bookmarks and liners to ⅛ and ¼ inch for boxes and most other projects. Typical good choices include birch- and poplar-faced plywood. If plywood is not available locally, contact Wildwood Designs, Inc., Richland Center, Wisconsin; this company carries plywood specially for scroll sawyers.

It is always important to check all stock thicknesses against the pattern. Often, metric-sized plywood, although sold in fractional sizes, will be slightly under (or over) the dimension specified by the supplier. It may be necessary to modify your pattern slightly to allow for these inconsistencies.

Transferring Patterns to the Wood

Transferring patterns to material for sawing can certainly be done in traditional ways, such as tracing with carbon or graphite papers. However, the new technique only involves the following steps: 1. copying the pattern directly from the book on an office-quality copy machine, at which time it can be enlarged or reduced as desired; 2. cutting out the pattern with a pair of scissors to a rough size; 3. coating the back of the pattern with a very light mist of temporary-bonding spray adhesive (Illus. 5); and 4. hand-pressing the pattern copy directly onto the workpiece.

Temporary-bonding spray adhesives are available at crafts shops and from mail-order sources. One kind we use is 3-M's Spray Mount adhesive, but other brands work equally well. Some craftspeople prefer using a brush-on application of rubber cement for securing patterns to the workpiece. This is an effective technique only when you are working with small paper patterns.

Before using the adhesive, test it on scrap first. To use the spray adhesive, simply spray a very light mist onto the back of the pattern copy; do *not* spray it on the wood. Wait 10 to 30 seconds, and then press the pattern onto the workpiece. It should maintain contact with the workpiece during sawing. After all the cutting is completed, the paper pattern should peel very easily and cleanly from the workpiece (Illus. 6). Should the pattern be difficult to remove because too much adhesive was used, simply wipe the top of the pattern with a rag slightly dampened in solvent.

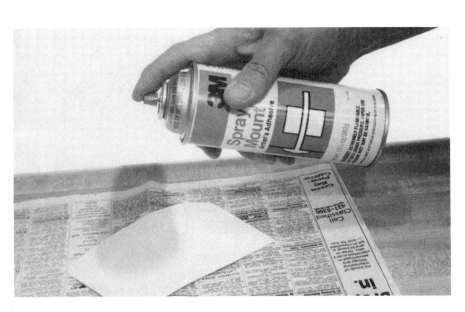

Illus. 5. Applying a sparse coating of adhesive to the back of a photocopied pattern.

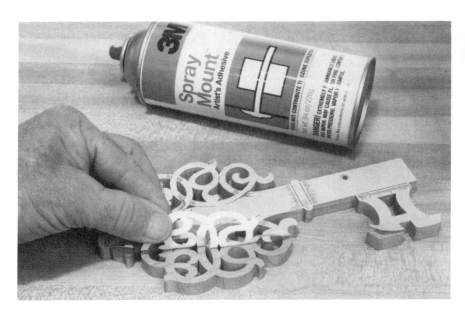

Illus. 6. After the sawing is completed, the pattern should peel off the surface very easily.

Stack-Sawing

Stack- or plural-cutting is a basic production technique that should not be overlooked whenever a quantity of the same cutout is required. It involves sawing two or more layers of materials at the same time. Very thin plywood can be stacked in many layers and cut all at once. (Refer to Illus. I-5, page 10, and page 34, which show the stacking of seventeen ⅟₃₂-inch plywood bookmarks.) Sometimes scroll sawyers will use an inexpensive, low-grade material as a bottom layer to prevent saw-blade tear-out, or feathering, from occurring on the bottom or exit side of the project itself.

You can hold together layers in various ways while they are being sawn; this includes nailing or tacking, spot-gluing in the waste areas, and using double-faced tape. If you want to tack layers of thin plywood together, place the stack on top of a steel plate. The nails will peen themselves just as they reach through the bottom layer. Touch them up with a file if necessary.

It is important that you carefully analyze each project before stack-cutting its parts. There are some projects that require bevel cuts or slanting slots (mortises) that must be made with the saw table tilted. You *cannot* stack and cut multiple parts with the table tilted. Of course, in some cases you can stack-cut with the table perpendicular to the blade. However, this method works only with those projects that have slightly angular tab-and-slot assemblies. You may need to cut the slots slightly wider than usual or file one inside wall of the slot or mortise to allow the tab to slip in at the necessary angle. In some cases, the angular penetration of the tab into a straight slot pinches the parts in position somewhat like a "snap fit," thus holding the assembly tightly without the need for glue or nails. Two project examples with slight angular assemblies but that also may have some parts stack-cut are the wheelbarrow and carriage projects shown in Illus. 7 and 8.

Surface Embellishment

A number of designs allow for optional surface embellishment of basic relief carving or wood-burned detailing. Illus. 9 shows key racks with wood-burned line detail and with no surface detail. Illus. I-1 on page 8 shows a surface-carved key rack. If nothing

Illus. 7. Using a small file to enlarge a mortise slot opening. Employ a similar technique to modify slot or mortise angles when necessary, for perfect fits.

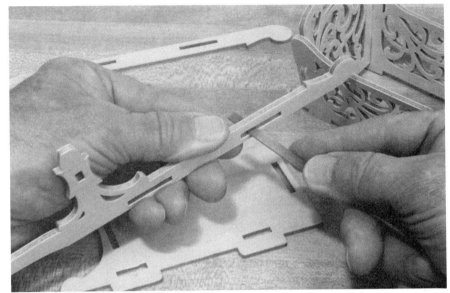

Illus. 8. The sides of this carriage with their bottom slots were stack-cut with the blade at 90 degrees to the table, but in theory the slots should be sawn individually at slight bevels.

Illus. 9. Above: A project without any surface detailing. Below: A project with wood-burned line detailing.

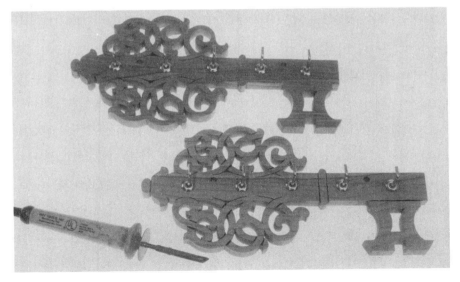

is done to the face surface at all, the project still looks good. Wood-burning line detail is very easy to do. This technique is recommended when plywood is used, but wood-burning is not required with or limited to just plywood surfaces.

Carving surface embellishment on solid wood is also very easy to do. Carved low-relief surfaces add an intriguing dimension to the project and accentuate the overall design.

Illus. 10–17 show some techniques involved in wood-burning or carving a face surface.

Illus. 10. After sawing the piece and removing the pattern, pencil in the over and under marks for wood-burning or carving.

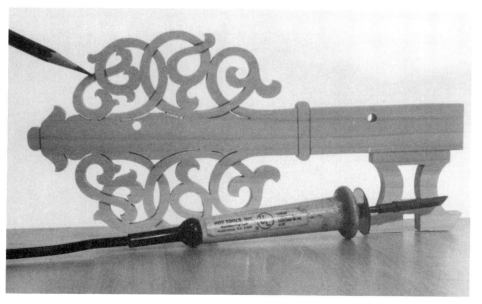

Illus. 11. Use a burning tool such as this and burn in the pencil lines.

Illus. 12. The wood-burn-ing in process.

Illus. 13. With the blade held vertically, sever the wood fibres by cutting along the pencil lines.

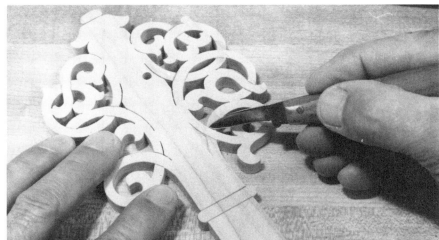

Illus. 14. Making a slicing cut to lift and cut a chip.

Illus. 15. Slicing across the grain.

Illus. 16. Slanting or tapering the surfaces inward to a depth of about 1/16 inch is all that's required to obtain a good visual effect.

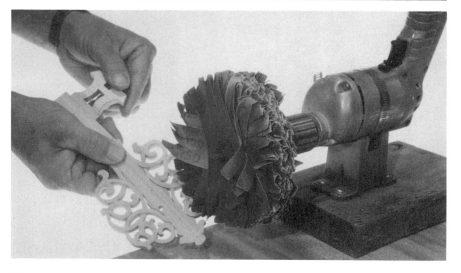

Illus. 17. Using a flutter-wheel abrasive to remove bottom-side feathering and to soften the sharply sawn and carved edges of the front surface.

Patterns and Projects

Viking ship and horse.

Small cutouts.

Small cutouts.

Small cutouts.

Small cutouts.

Small cutouts.

Billy goat sun catcher.

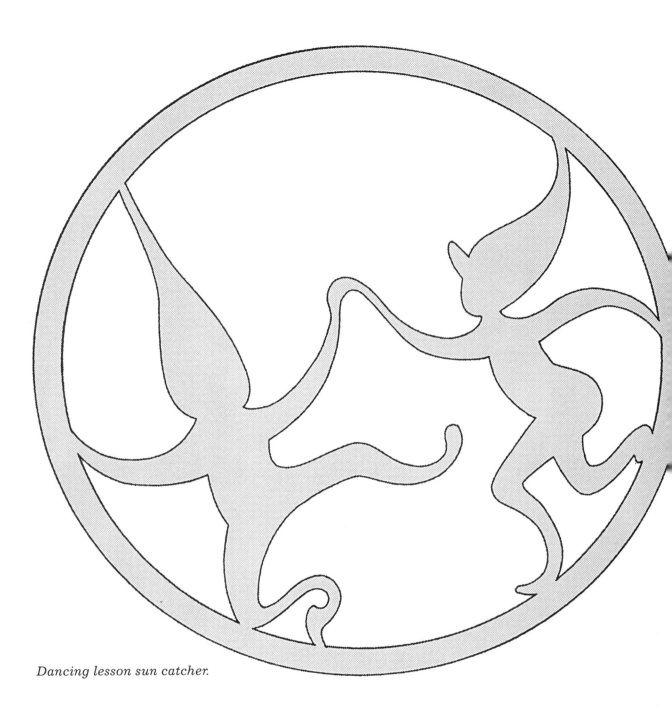

Dancing lesson sun catcher.

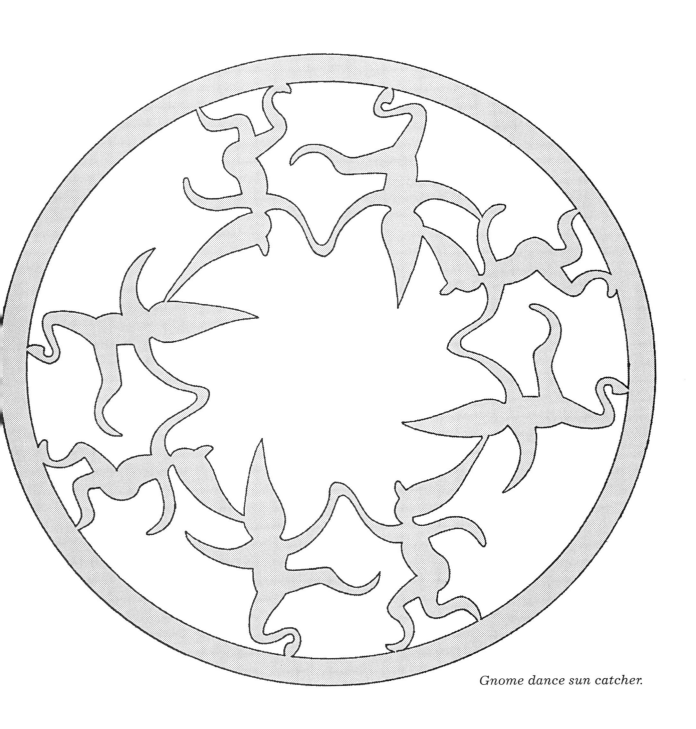

Gnome dance sun catcher.

A. B.

Parrot sun catcher.

32

Right: A clock of unfinished plywood and a painted Swedish candle holder. Below: A solid-wood puzzle, a cutout, a hanging plywood ornament depicting the character Nils Holgersson, and eardrops of solid wood.

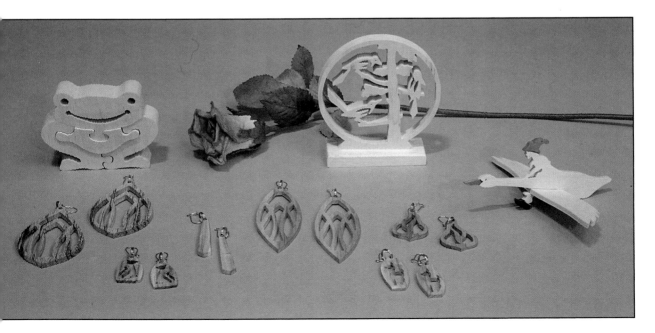

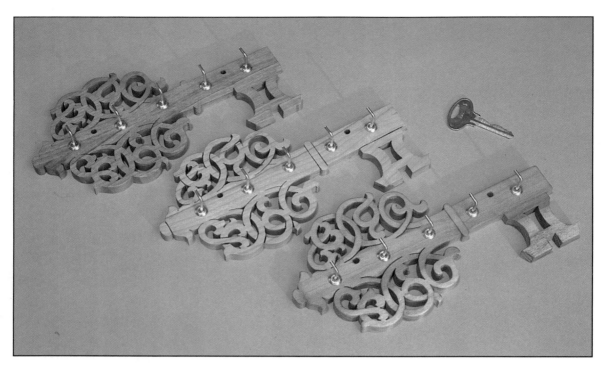

Above: Comparing three surface options. From top to bottom: A plain surface, a wood-burned surface with line detail, and a carved, embellished surface. Below: Wheelbarrow components with typical sawn slots and tabs ready for assembly.

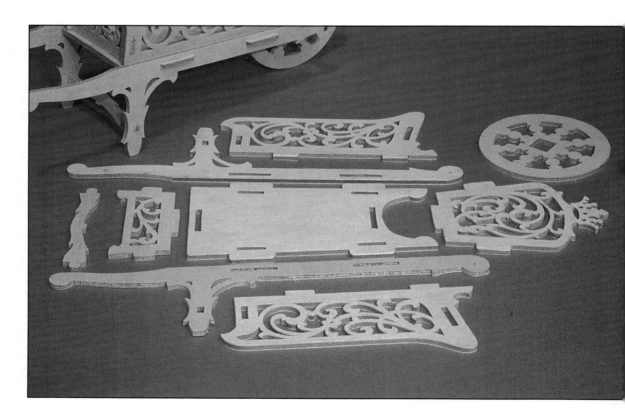

B

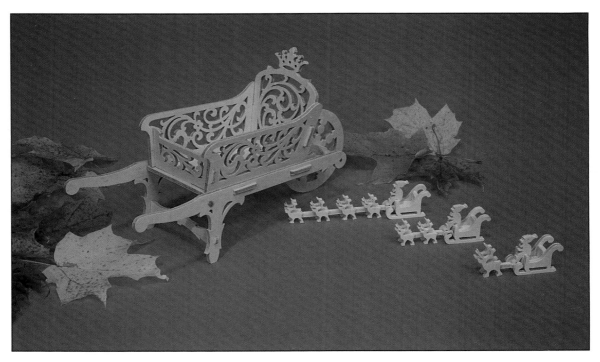

Above: An assembled wheelbarrow and some mini-ornaments. Below: A variety of mini-cutouts and ornaments with a Viking ship clock.

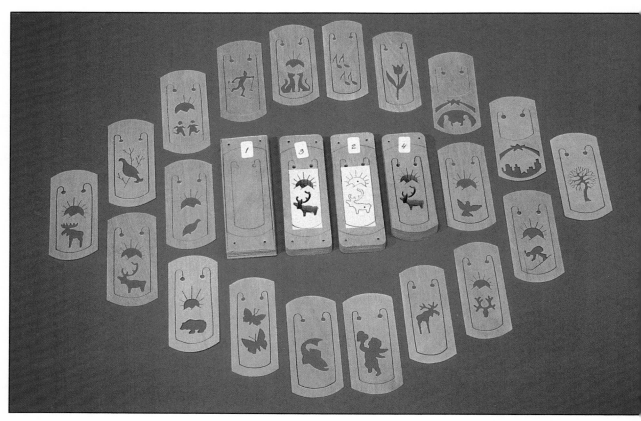

Above: Sample bookmarks showing the essential steps of making bookmarks, surrounded by a variety of different designs. Below: More bookmark designs and a "point of purchase" display rack.

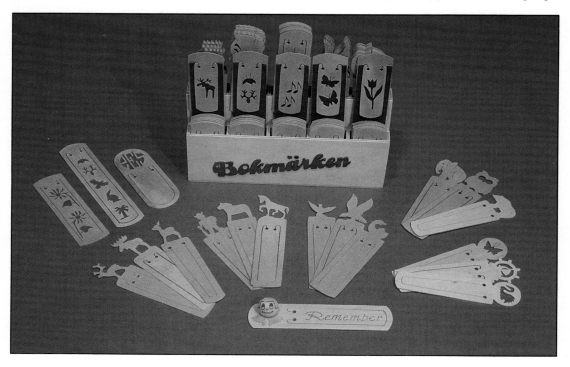

D

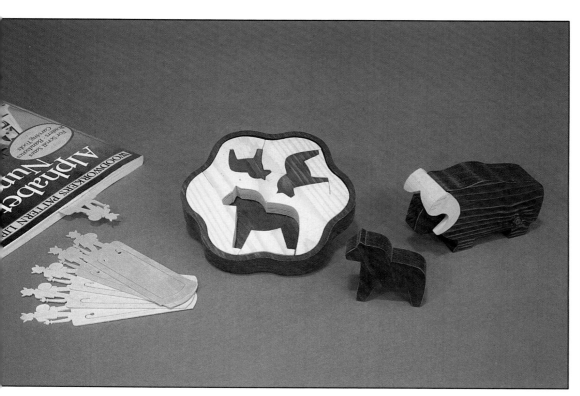

Above: Bookmarks, a horse-tray puzzle, and a musk-ox. Below: A variety of candle holders and a herd of mini-cutouts.

A trinket box made of ⅛-inch-thick plywood.

A flower-vase holder that features halved joints and typical slot-and-tab assembly.

A small berry basket.

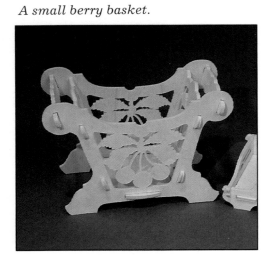

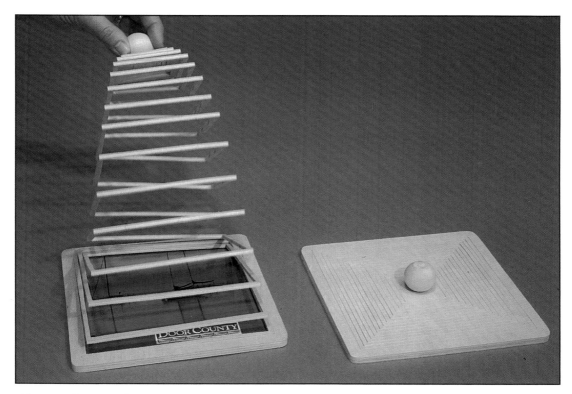

Above: This novelty project made of ⅛-inch-thick plywood yields a surprise message or advertisement when stretched open. Below: Elegant six-piece candle holders sawn from scrap pine.

Above: A flowerpot surround made of snap-together pine slats, and a decorative fret-work carriage. Below: A variety of projects incorporating components produced by a novel, parallel-cutting pattern in which each sawn part is glued to another in an extended or open position.

Bookmarks cut from thin plywood produce good sales in gift, book, and stationery stores.

A variety of longer bookmarks, most of them with end designs.

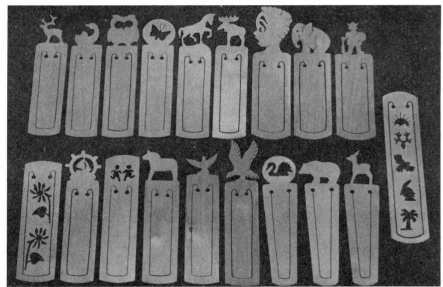

This novel "paper clip" was made using bookmark stock and sawing techniques.

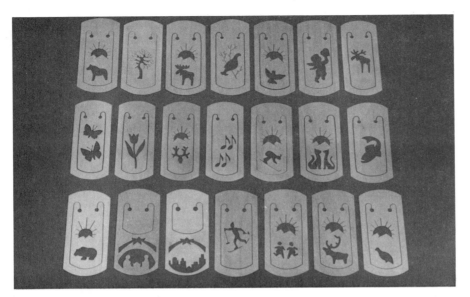

A selection of shorter bookmarks with pierced designs.

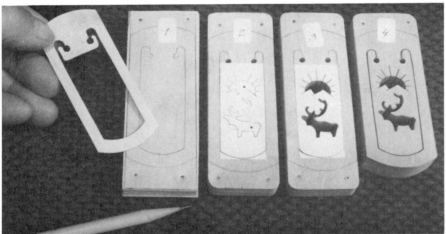

The general steps used to produce bookmarks in quantity. From left to right: 1. stack and tack 17 or 18 layers of $\frac{1}{32}$-inch plywood cut to a rough width, and mark the holes and slit with a template; 2. apply the pattern design, drill holes, and sand the bookmark to a finished width; 3. make interior cuts; and 4. saw and sand the first end, and cut the second end to shape.

An intriguing display rack such as this one generates interest and sales for a bookmark business.

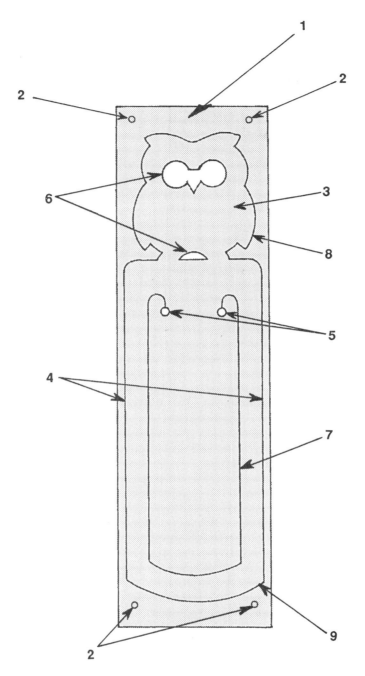

Bookmark-making procedures: 1. saw $\frac{1}{32}$"-thin birch plywood stock to rough width and length; 2. stack and tack up to 17 or 18 layers, depending upon the cutting capabilities of the saw; 3. draw the design or adhere a paper pattern to the stack; 4. work the stack to finished width using a disc or belt sander; 5. drill $\frac{1}{8}$-inch holes for the slit; 6. drill as required for internal openings; 7. cut the slit with a No. 12 blade; and 8. cut the saw design figure with a No. 3 to No. 5 blade.

Bookmark shapes with pierced designs.

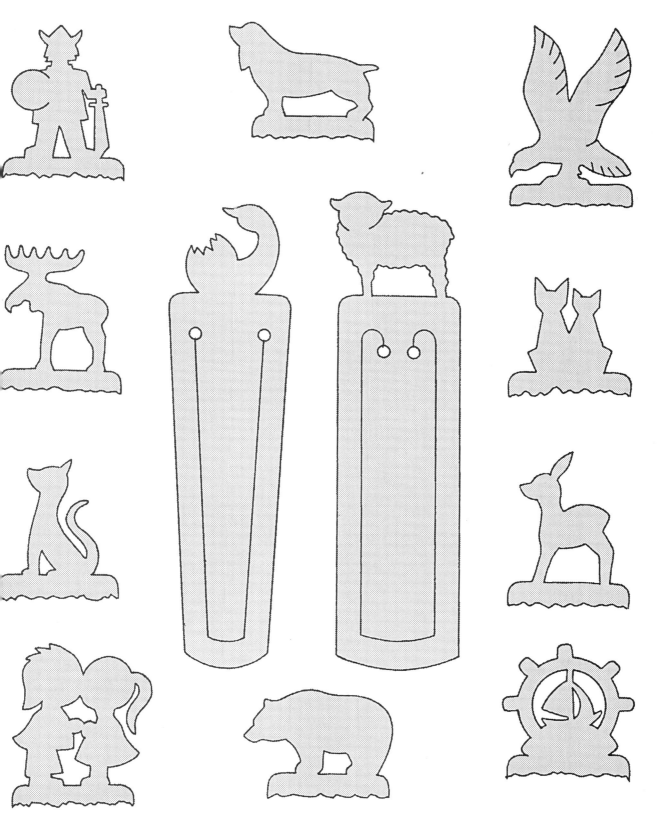

Bookmark designs with various end designs.

More end designs for bookmarks.

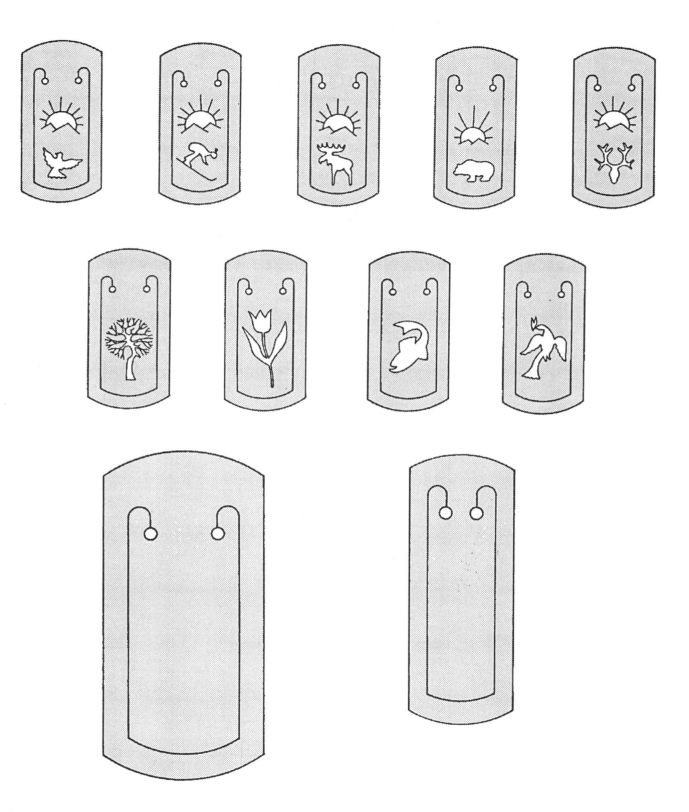

Shorter bookmarks. Note: The top nine designs are half the recommended size. Enlarge them 200 percent.

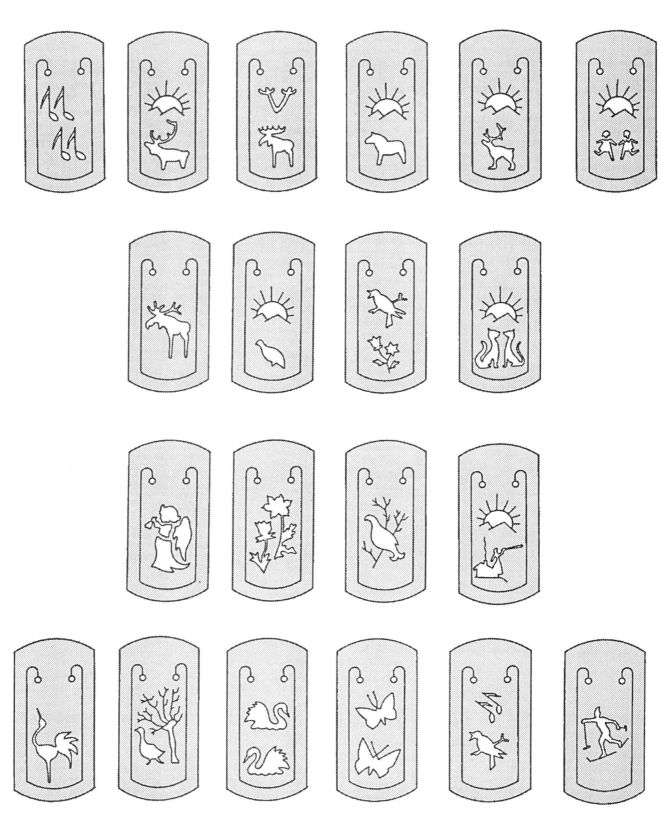

More half-size designs. Enlarge them 200 percent.

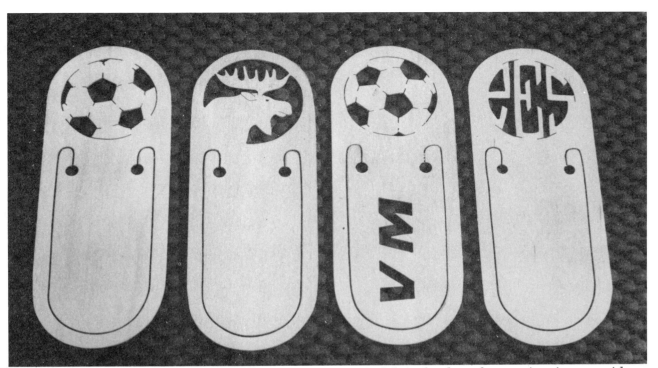

The designs of these bookmarks may inspire more ideas.

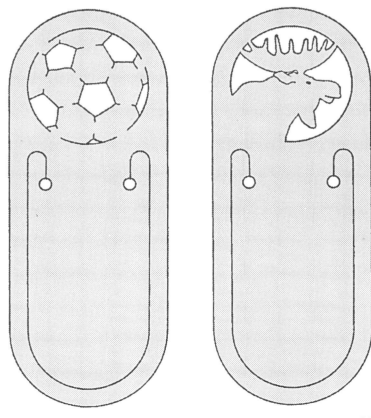

Full-size bookmark patterns.

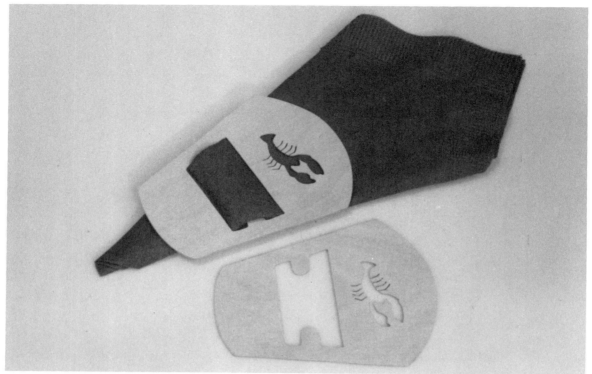

Many of the pierced designs for the bookmarks can also be used for these delightful paper napkin holders.

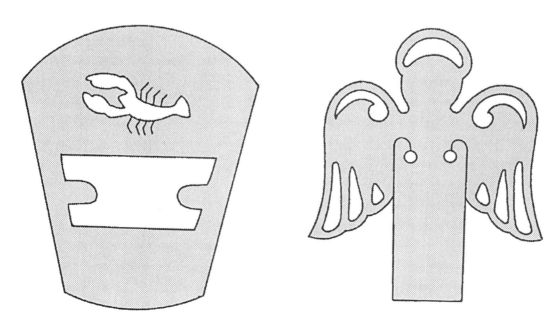

At left: A napkin holder full-size pattern. At right: An angel bookmark full-size pattern.

Shelf full-size pattern for ⅛-inch material.

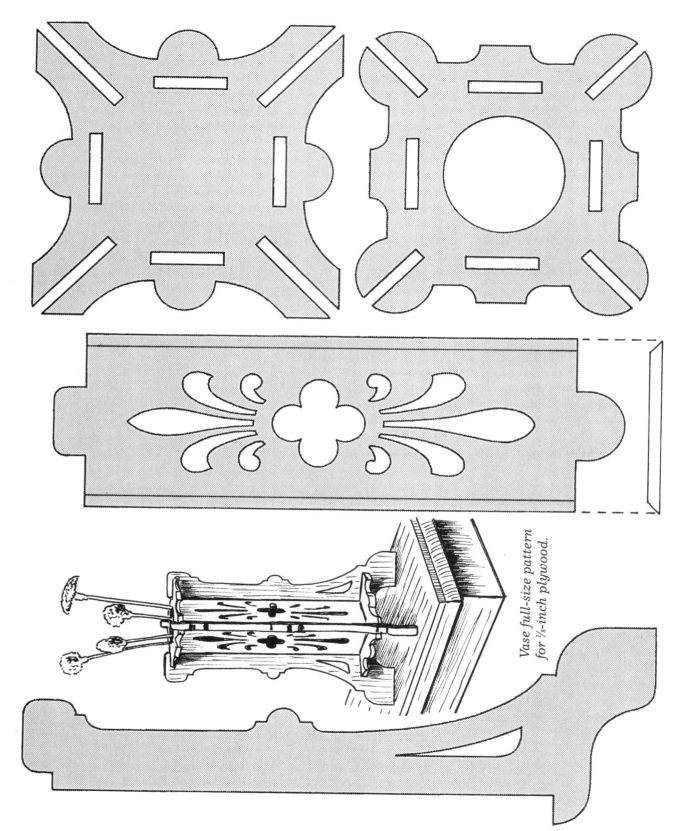

Vase full-size pattern for ⅛-inch plywood.

44

Trivet full-size pattern for ¼-inch material.

45

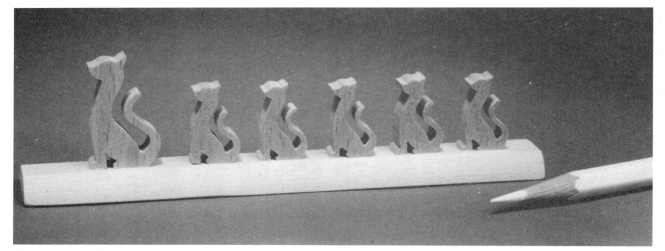

A series of mini-cutouts glued to a flattened dowel.

Mini-fawn cutouts glued to a thin cross section of a tree branch.

A herd of mini-deer cutouts glued to a diagonally cut section of a tree branch.

46

Mini-cutouts.

47

Three-dimensional ornaments created with various mini-patterns sawn from thin plywood.

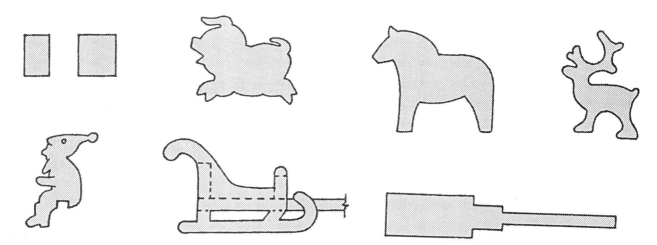

Three-dimensional ornament full-size patterns.

48

Moose family.

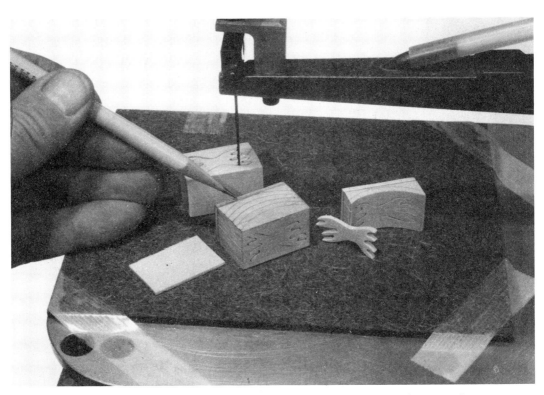

Compound-sawing produces the curved antlers. First, cut out the top-view pro-file. Then glue it and the waste to a thin backer (plywood) as shown at glue line (under the pencil point). Finally, saw the curved front-view profile as shown at the right. Tip: A piece of hardboard taped to the saw table eliminates or reduces the size of the table opening around the blade.

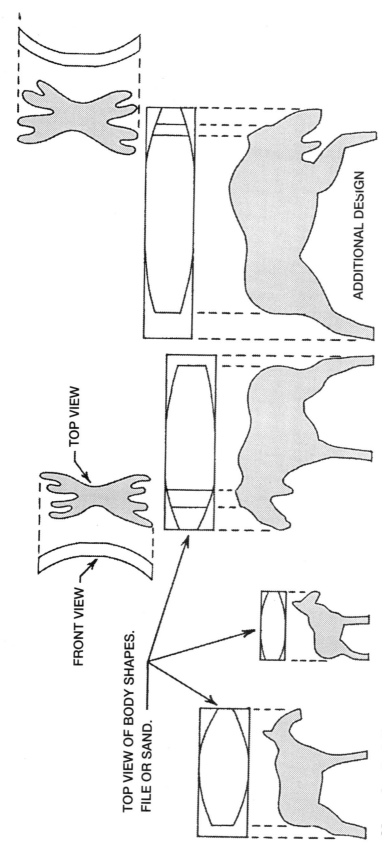

TOP VIEW

FRONT VIEW

TOP VIEW OF BODY SHAPES.
FILE OR SAND.

ADDITIONAL DESIGN

Moose family full-size patterns.

50

The Swedish figure of Nils Holgersson on his goose, from his "Wonderful Voyage through Sweden," is depicted in this hanging ornament. See page 52 for patterns.

Musk-ox. Stain its body the typical dark brown color of a musk-ox. See page 53 for pattern.

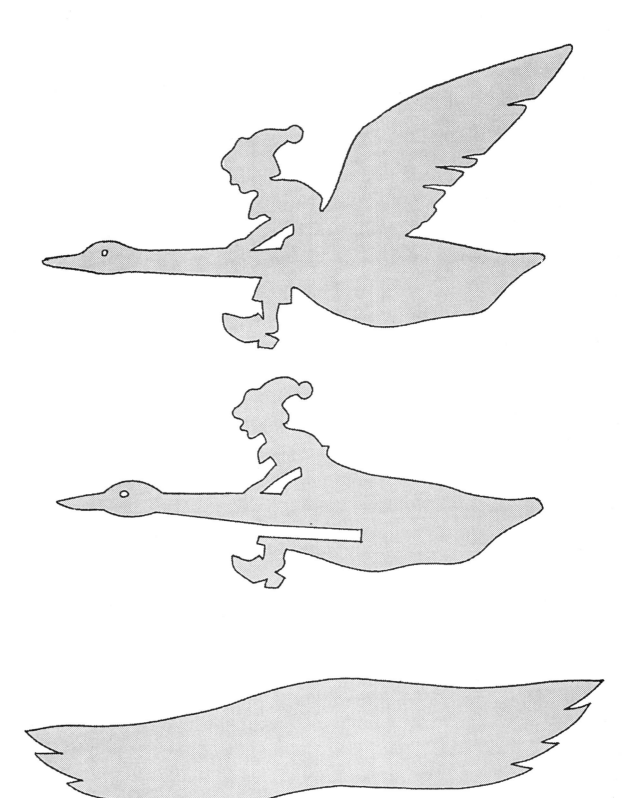

Hanging ornament full-size patterns.

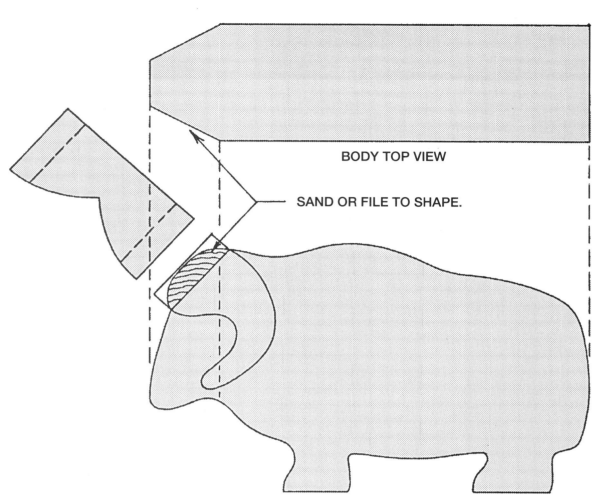

BODY TOP VIEW

SAND OR FILE TO SHAPE.

Musk-ox full-size pattern.

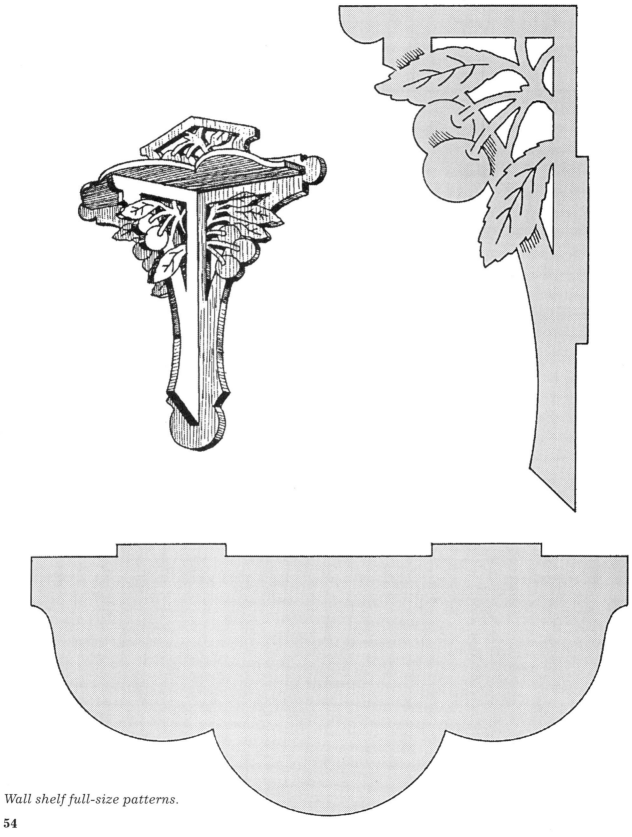

Wall shelf full-size patterns.

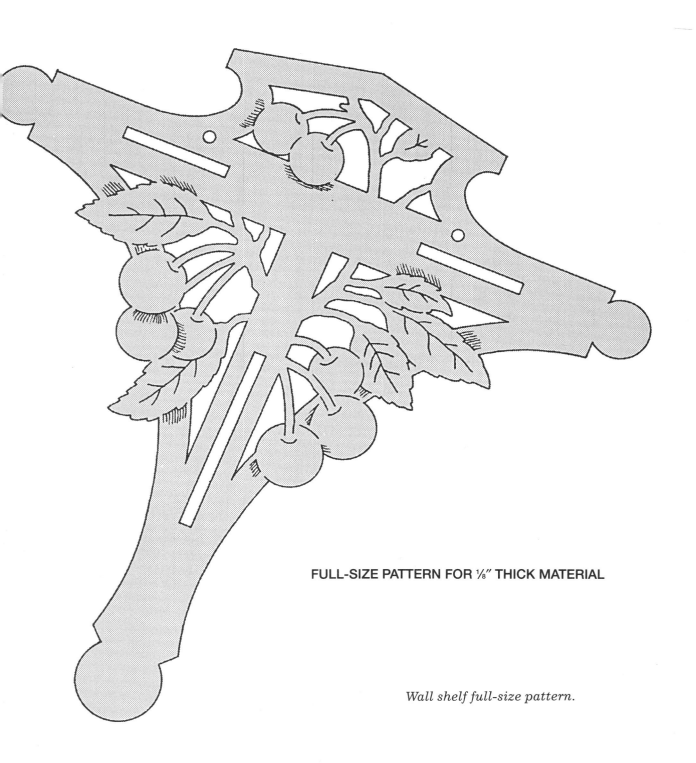

FULL-SIZE PATTERN FOR ⅛″ THICK MATERIAL

Wall shelf full-size pattern.

Corner shelf half-size patterns for ⅜-inch stock. Enlarge them 200 percent.

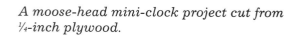

A moose-head mini-clock project cut from ¼-inch plywood.

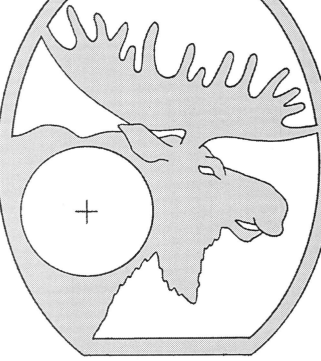

Moose-head clock full-size patterns.

Viking ship with a mini-clock

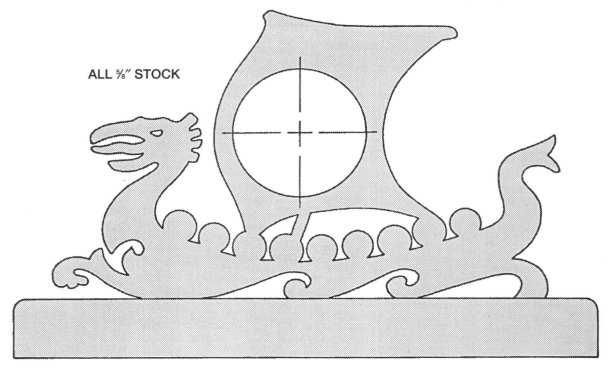

ALL ⅝″ STOCK

BASE, ⅝″ × 1¾″ × 6″

Viking ship with clock full-size pattern.

58

Key rack full-size pattern.

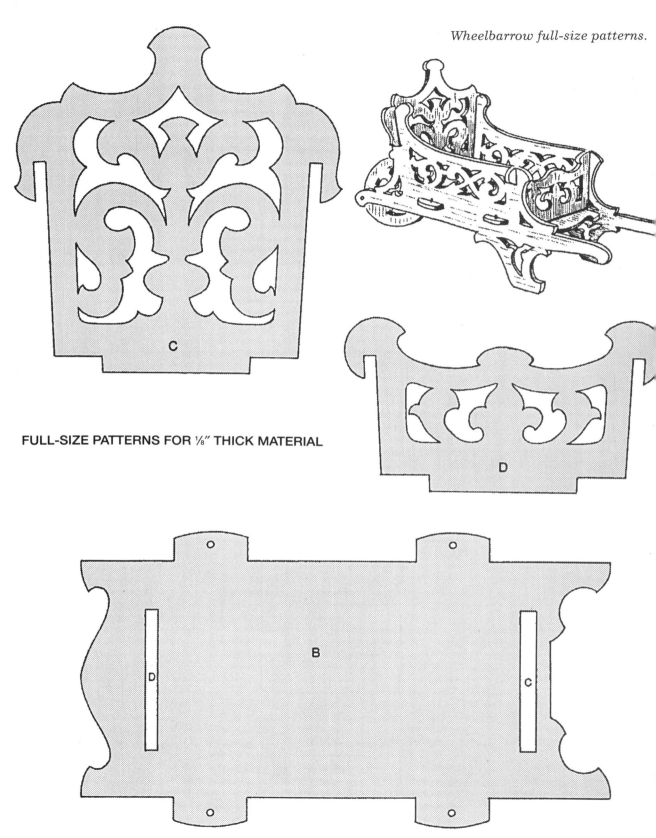

Wheelbarrow full-size patterns.

C

FULL-SIZE PATTERNS FOR ⅛″ THICK MATERIAL

D

D   B   C

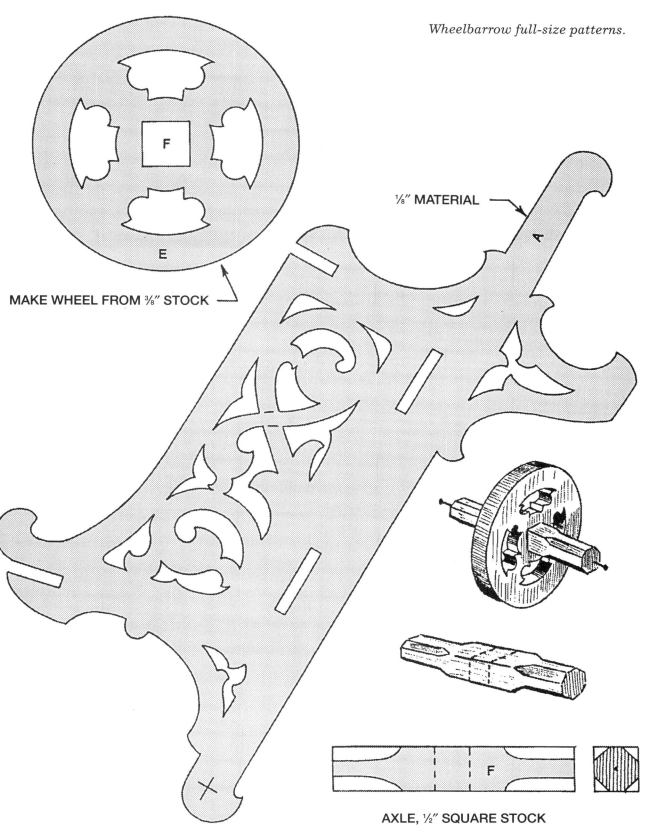

Wheelbarrow full-size patterns.

⅛" MATERIAL

MAKE WHEEL FROM ⅜" STOCK

AXLE, ½" SQUARE STOCK

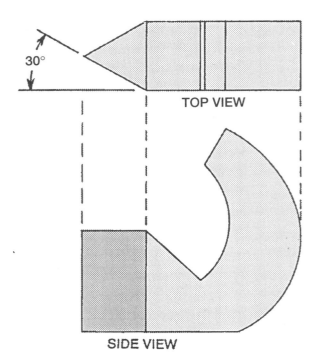

30°

TOP VIEW

SIDE VIEW

Full-size patterns for the candle holder. Make six identical pieces.

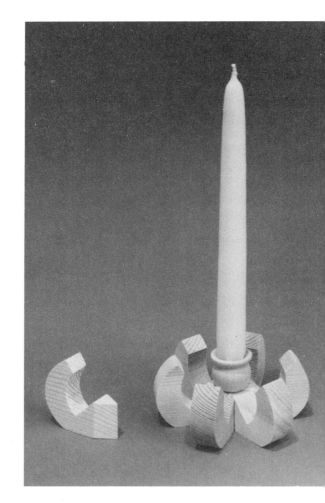

This six-piece candle holder is elegant in its simplicity.

Another project designed for holding a warming candle.

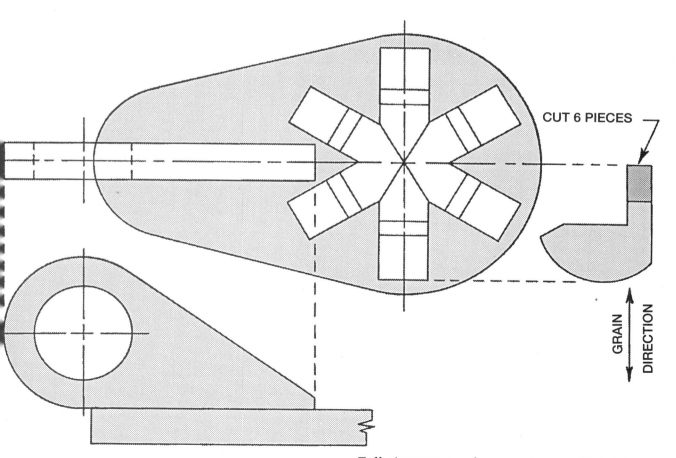

CUT 6 PIECES

GRAIN
DIRECTION

Full-size patterns for warming-candle holder.

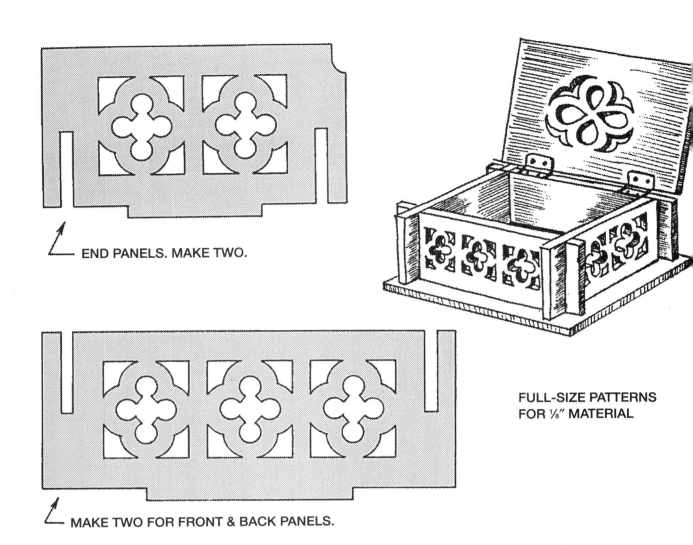

END PANELS. MAKE TWO.

FULL-SIZE PATTERNS
FOR ⅛″ MATERIAL

MAKE TWO FOR FRONT & BACK PANELS.

PATTERN FOR BASE
AND LID. CUT SLOTS
IN THE BASE ONLY.

Small box patterns.

Basket half-size patterns. Enlarge the patterns 200 percent for ⅛-inch-thick material.

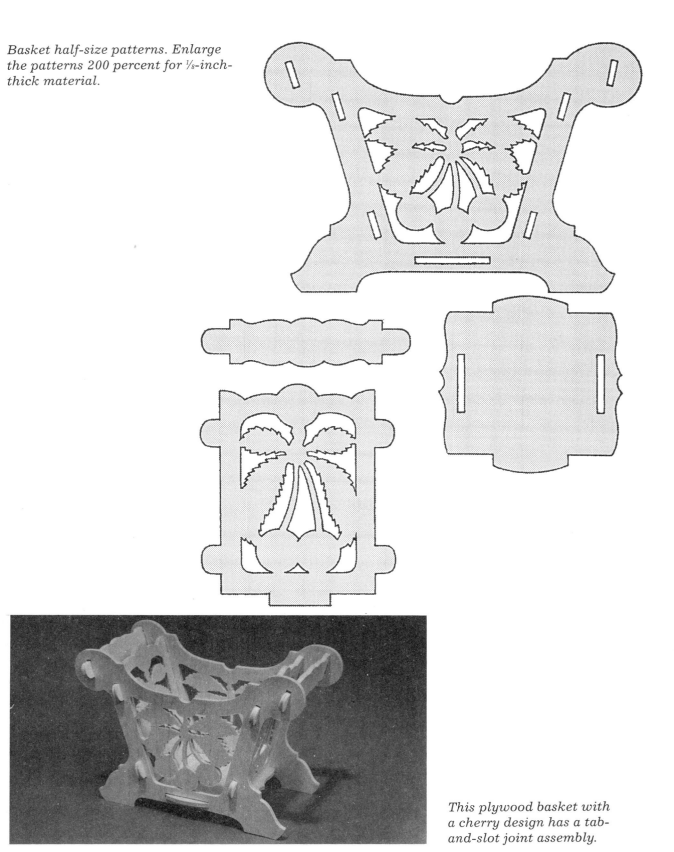

This plywood basket with a cherry design has a tab-and-slot joint assembly.

A simple frame. Make it to the size desired.

Wall shelf full-size patterns.

Wall shelf full-size pattern.

68

Horse tray puzzle. The pieces were sawn from solid wood. Stain the pieces after sawing them.

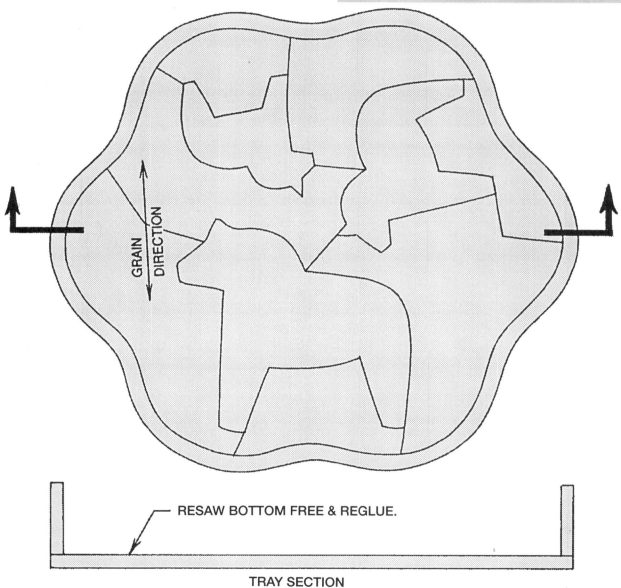

GRAIN DIRECTION

RESAW BOTTOM FREE & REGLUE.

TRAY SECTION

Horse-tray puzzle full-size patterns. Note: Use thin plywood for an optional bottom.

Full-size patterns for simple two-piece puzzles.

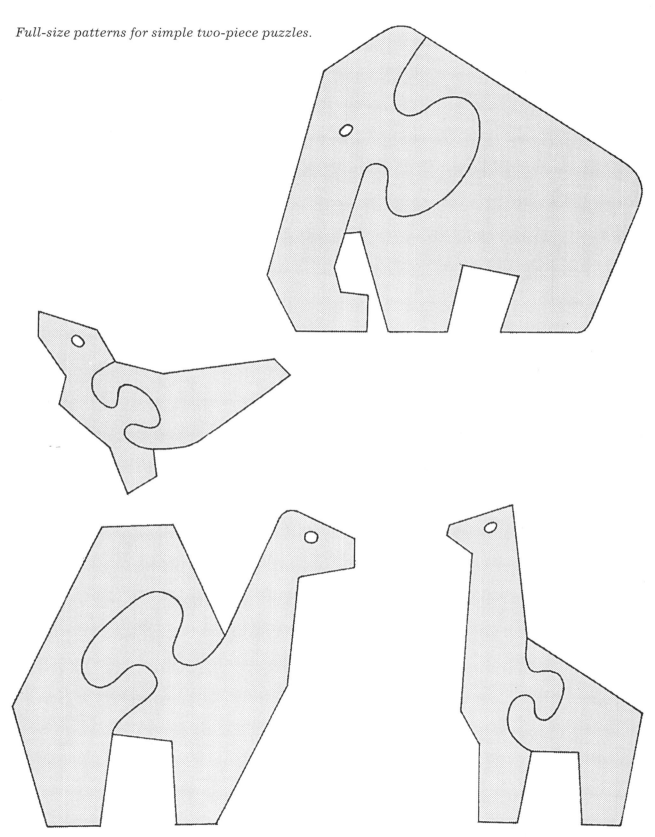

Standing frog puzzle.

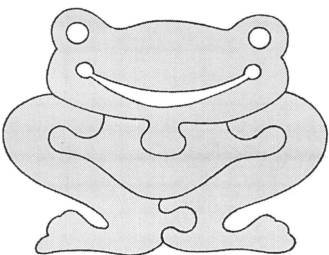

Standing frog puzzle full-size pattern.

CUT FROM ½″ TO 1″ THICK MATERIAL

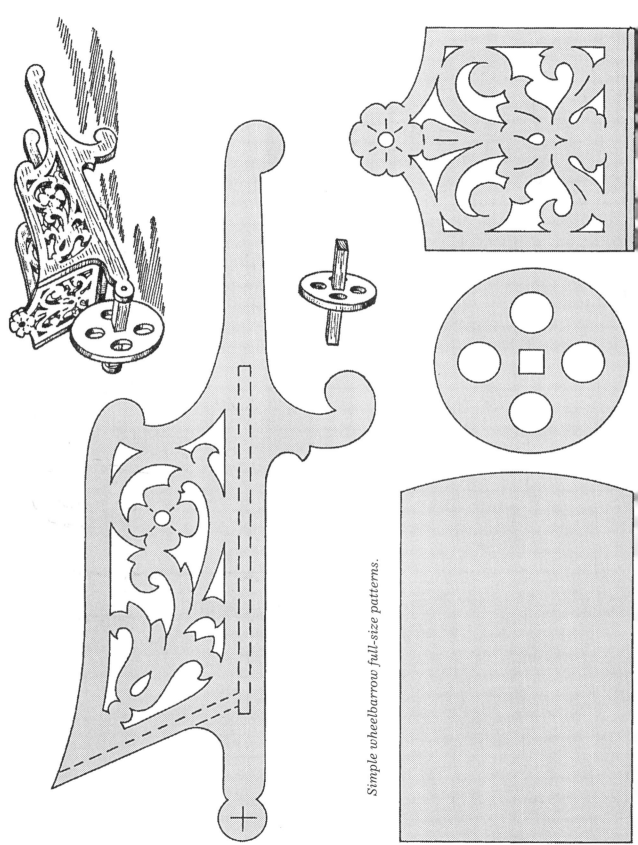

Simple wheelbarrow full-size patterns.

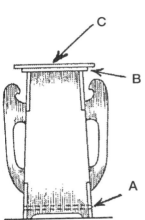

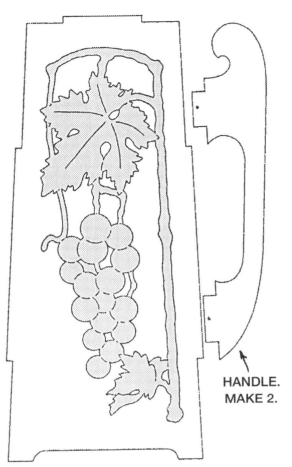

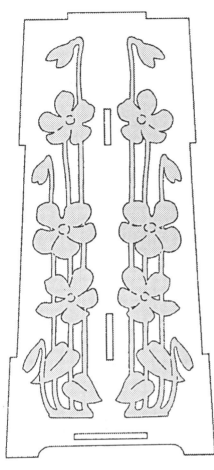

HANDLE.
MAKE 2.

FRONT & BACK WITH OVERLAY.
MAKE 2 EACH.

SIDES WITH OVERLAYS.
MAKE 2 EACH.

C

B

A

HALF-SIZE PATTERNS. ENLARGE 200% FOR ⅛" THICK MATERIAL.

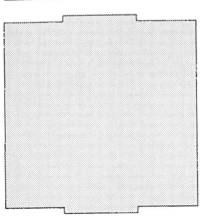

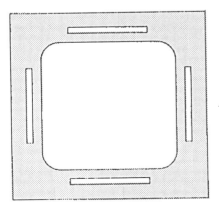

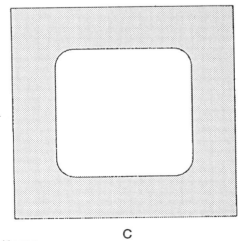

A

B

C

Vase patterns.

73

Deer shelf full-size pattern.

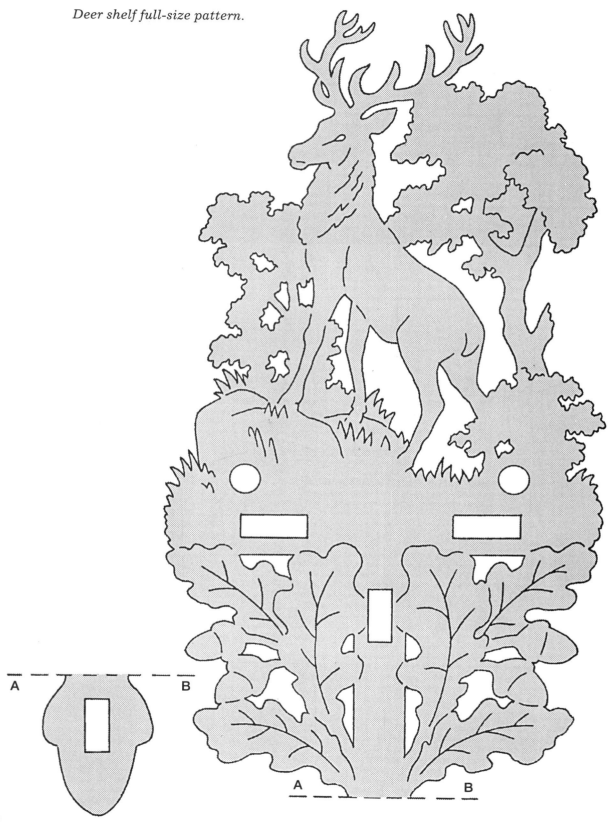

A   B

A   B

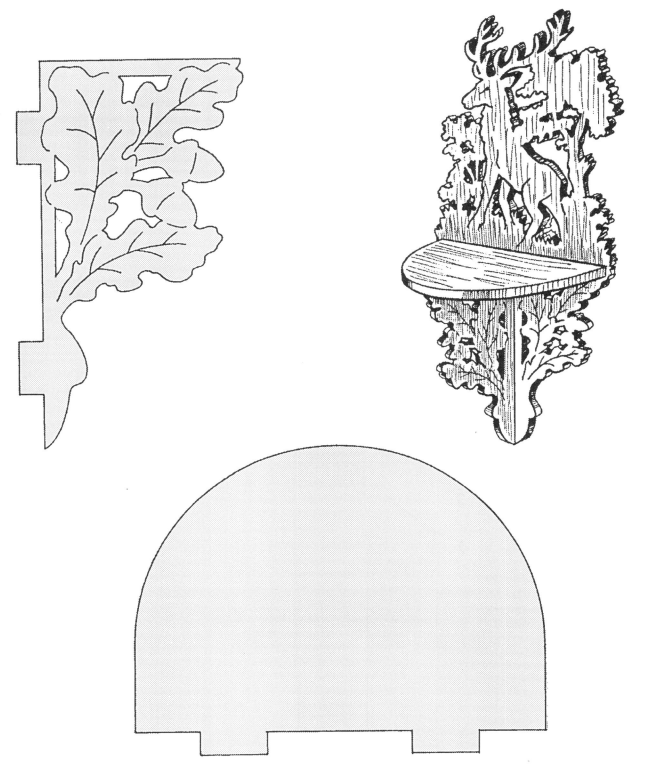

Deer shelf full-size patterns.

HALF-SIZE PATTERNS. ENLARGE 200% FOR ⅛" THICK MATERIAL.

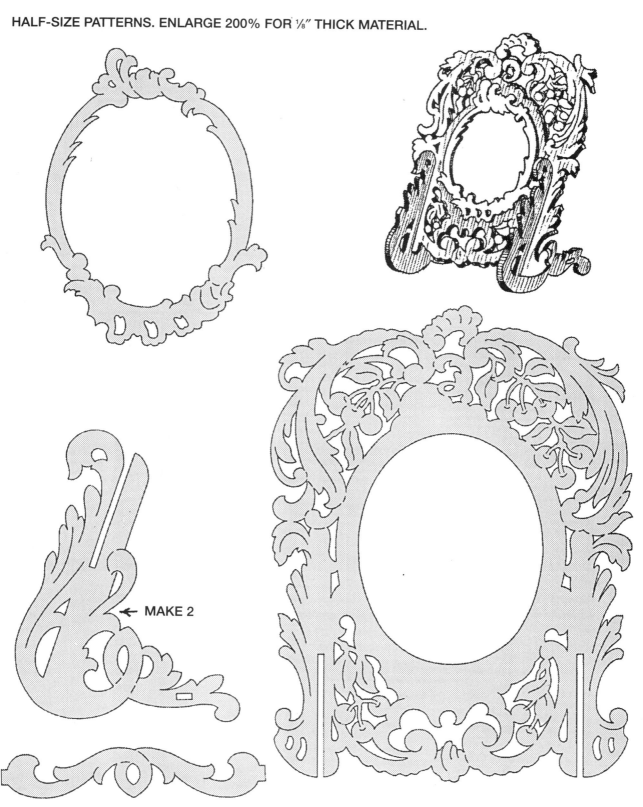

← MAKE 2

Standing photo frame half-size patterns.

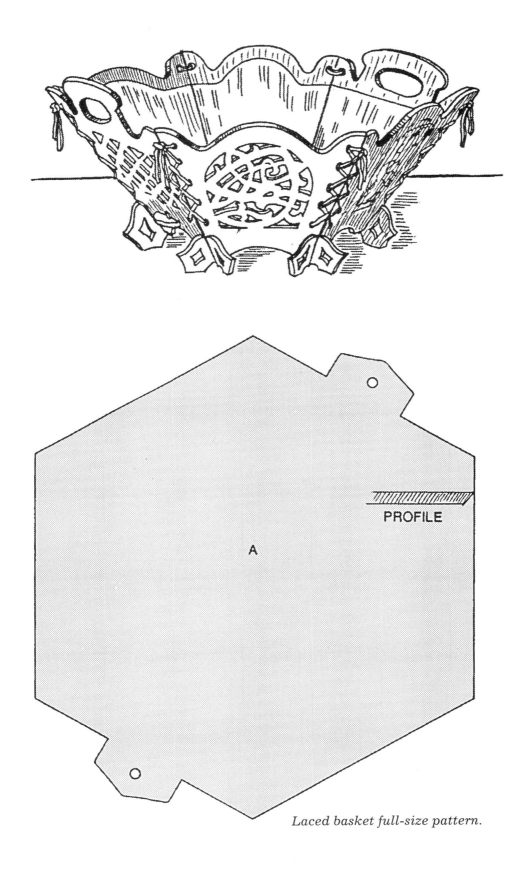

PROFILE

A

Laced basket full-size pattern.

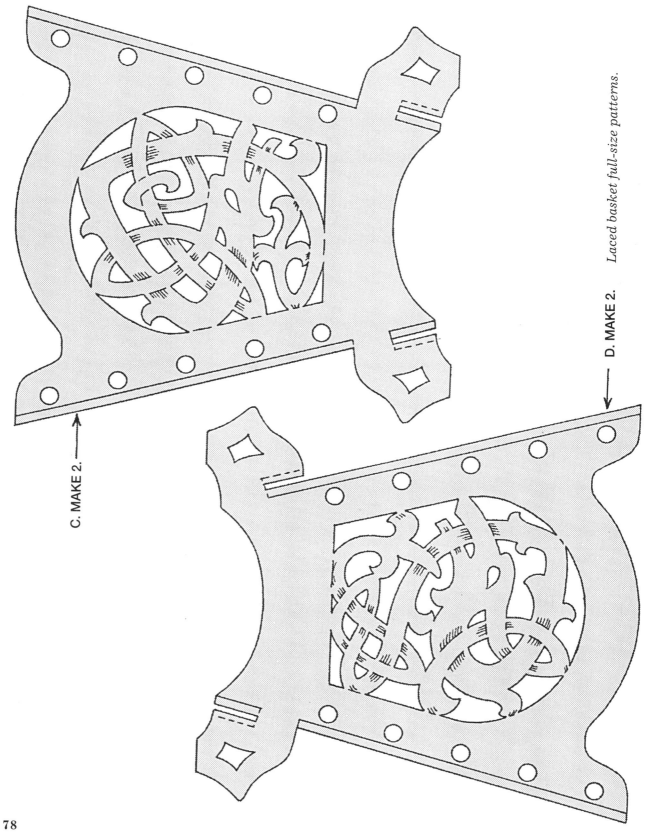

C. MAKE 2.

D. MAKE 2.

Laced basket full-size patterns.

78

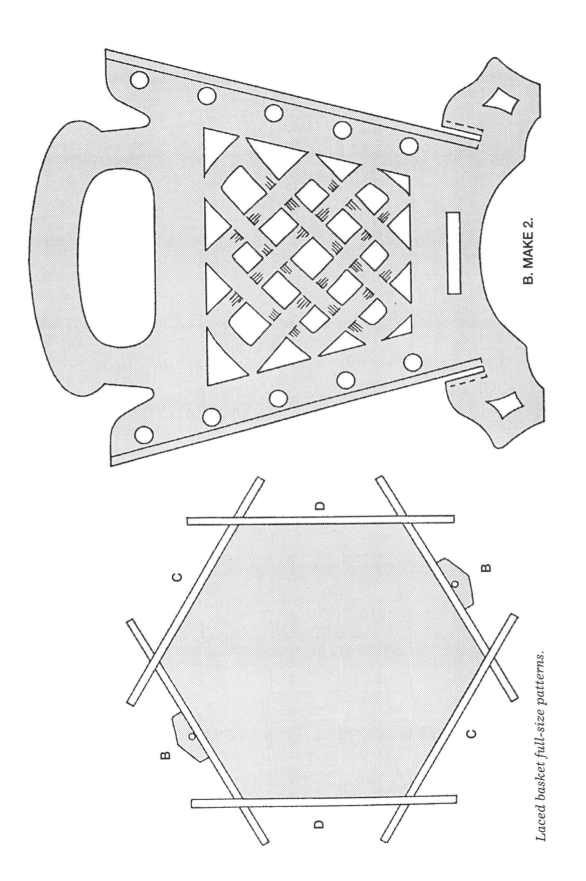

B. MAKE 2.

Laced basket full-size patterns.

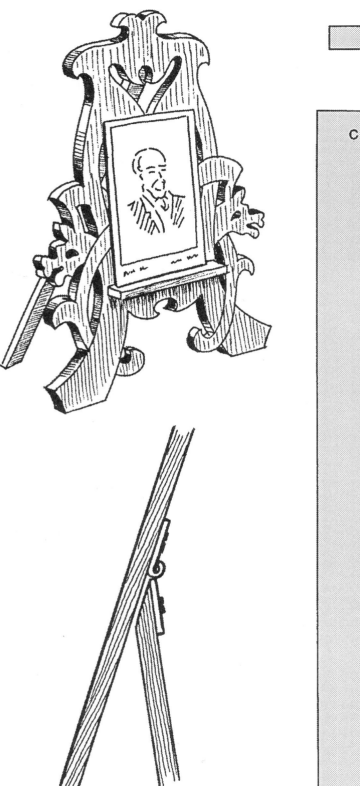

B

C

EDGE VIEW

Easel full-size patterns.

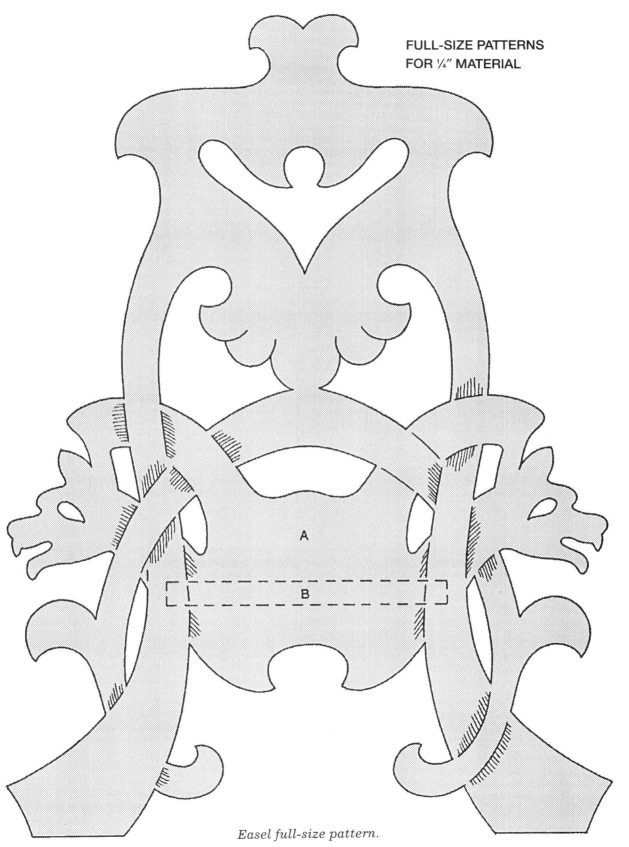

A

B

Easel full-size pattern.

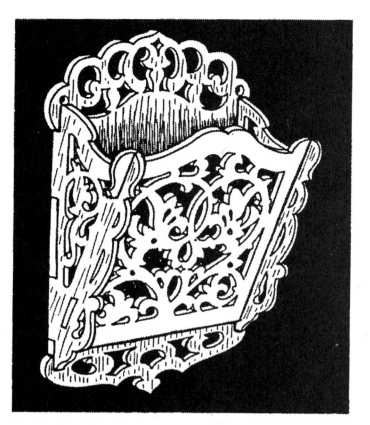

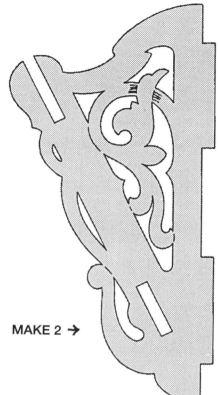

MAKE 2 →

Wall pocket half-size patterns.

HALF-SIZE PATTERN. ENLARGE 200% FOR ¼″ MATERIAL.

Wall pocket half-size pattern.

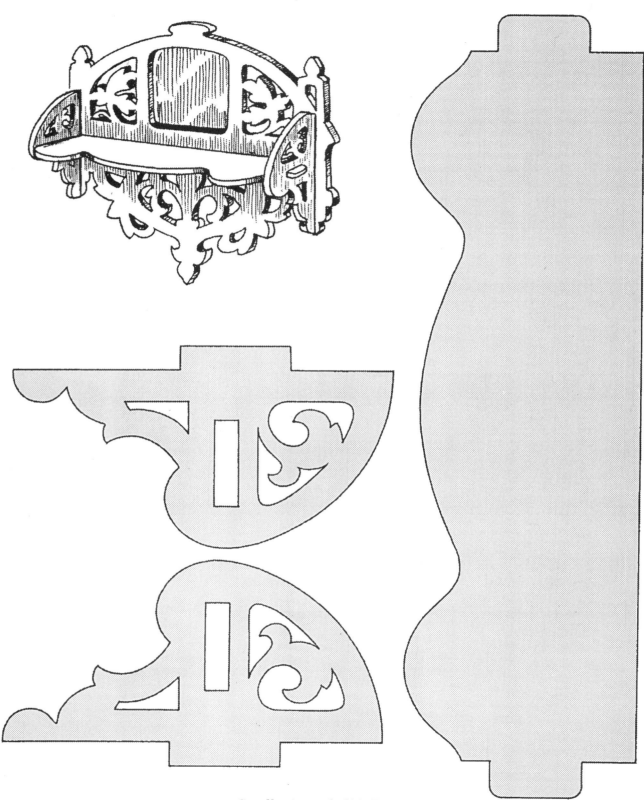

Small mirror shelf full-size patterns.

A

B

Small mirror shelf full-size half pattern.

85

A

B

Small mirror shelf full-size half pattern.

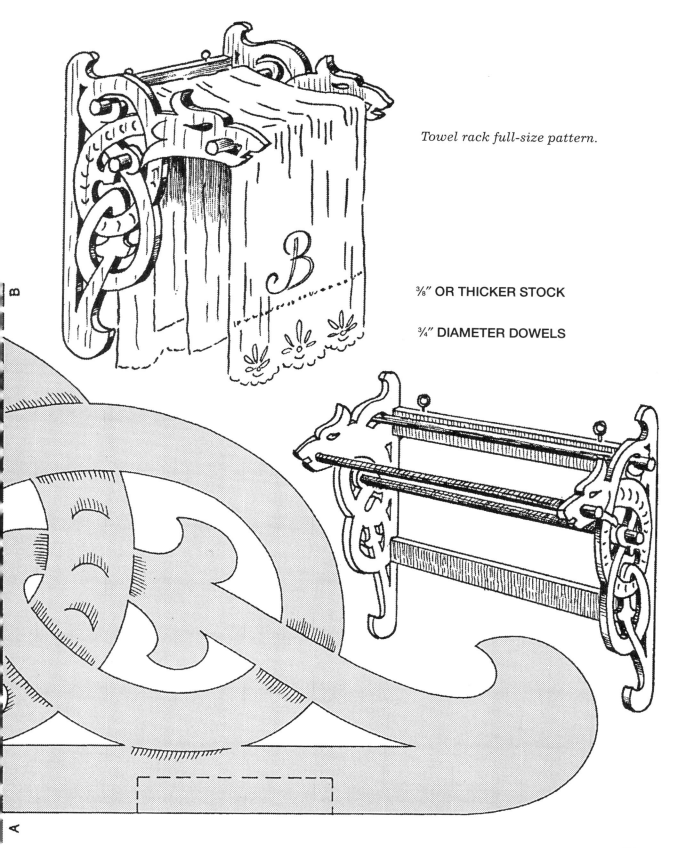

Towel rack full-size pattern.

⅜" OR THICKER STOCK

¾" DIAMETER DOWELS

Towel rack full-size pattern.

B

A

88

Double-photo frame half-size patterns.

OVERLAY

HALF-SIZE PATTERNS.
ENLARGE 200% FOR
⅛" THICK MATERIAL.

MAKE 2

Holder for large pillar-type candle.

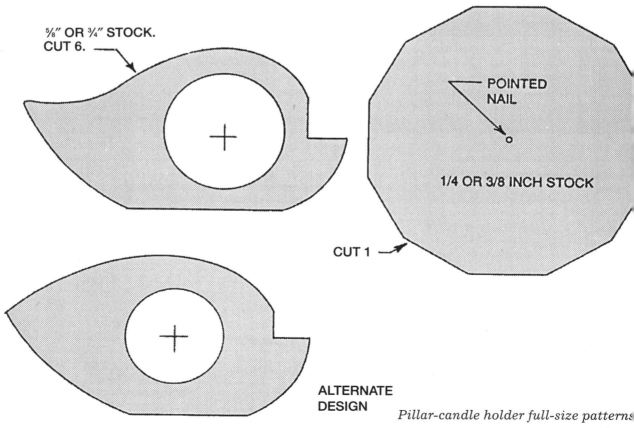

⅝" OR ¾" STOCK. CUT 6.

POINTED NAIL

1/4 OR 3/8 INCH STOCK

CUT 1

ALTERNATE DESIGN

Pillar-candle holder full-size patterns

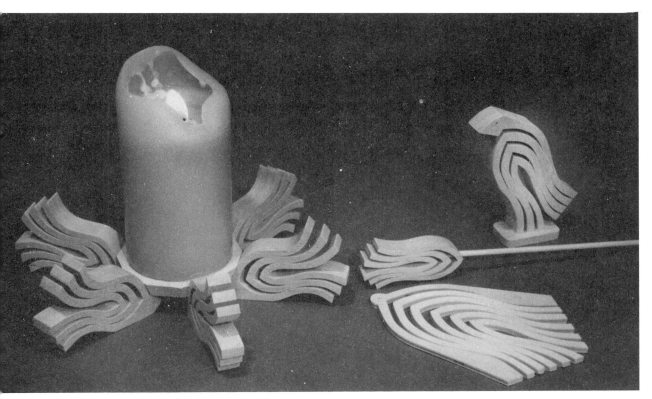

... variety of projects incorporating an unusual cutting concept that involves controlled shifting and ...uing of pieces made with parallel cuts.

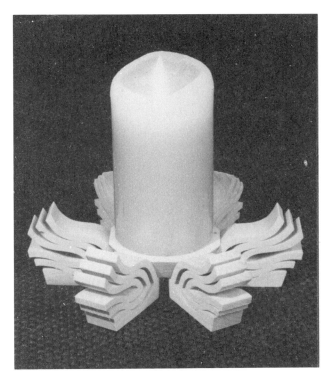

...his pillar-candle holder has six identical com-
...onents, each formed by the novel cutting tech-
...ique.

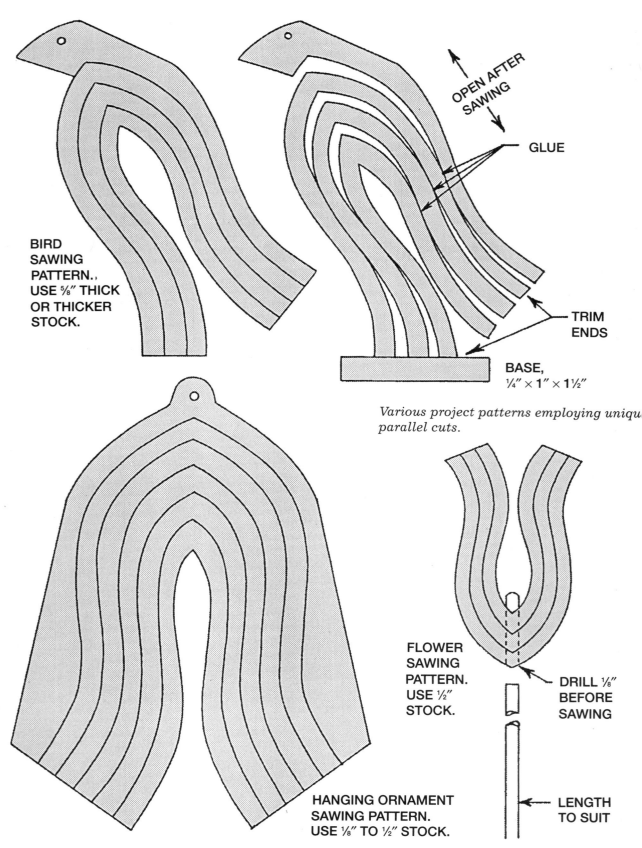

BIRD
SAWING
PATTERN.,
USE ⅝″ THICK
OR THICKER
STOCK.

OPEN AFTER
SAWING

GLUE

TRIM
ENDS

BASE,
¼″ × 1″ × 1½″

*Various project patterns employing uniqu(e)
parallel cuts.*

FLOWER
SAWING
PATTERN.
USE ½″
STOCK.

DRILL ⅛″
BEFORE
SAWING

HANGING ORNAMENT
SAWING PATTERN.
USE ⅛″ TO ½″ STOCK.

LENGTH
TO SUIT

Bottom view of pillar-candle holder.

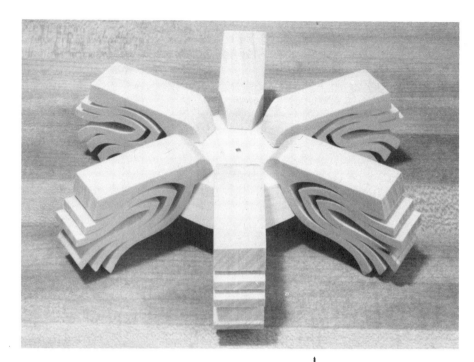

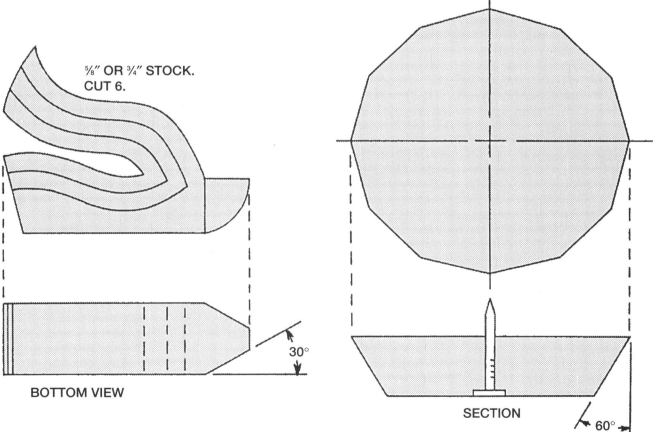

⅝″ OR ¾″ STOCK. CUT 6.

BOTTOM VIEW

30°

SECTION

60°

Pillar-candle holder full-size patterns.

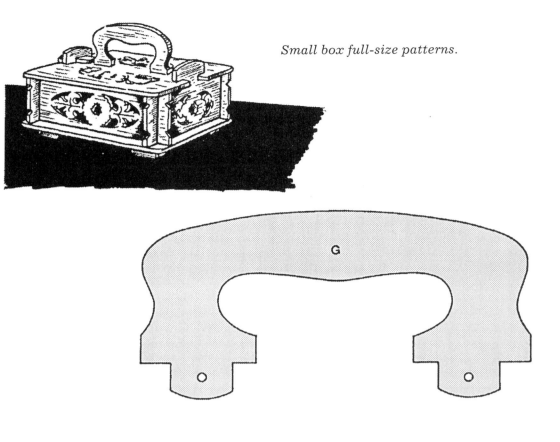

Small box full-size patterns.

G

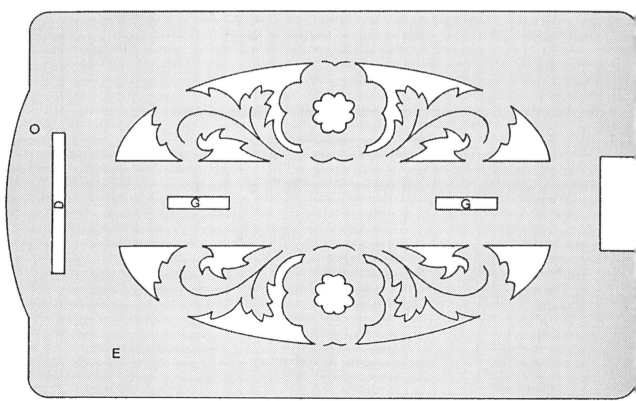

D

G

G

E

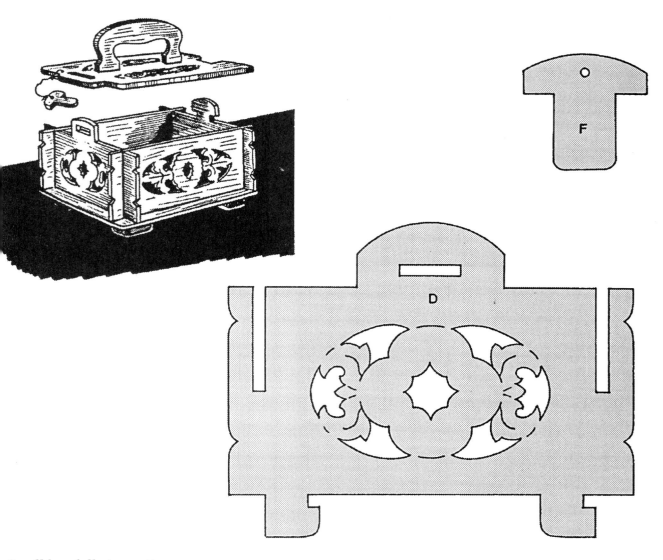

F

D

Small box full-size patterns.

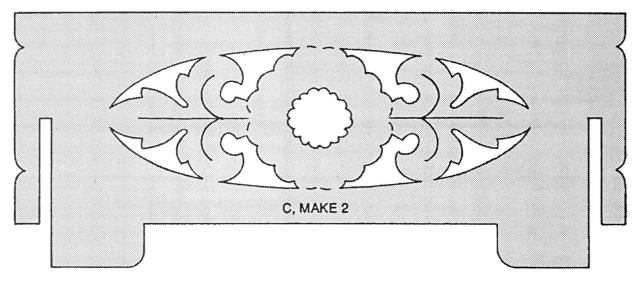

C, MAKE 2

**FULL-SIZE PATTERNS
FOR ⅛″ MATERIAL**

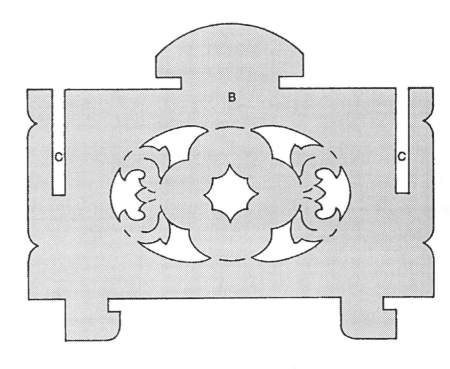

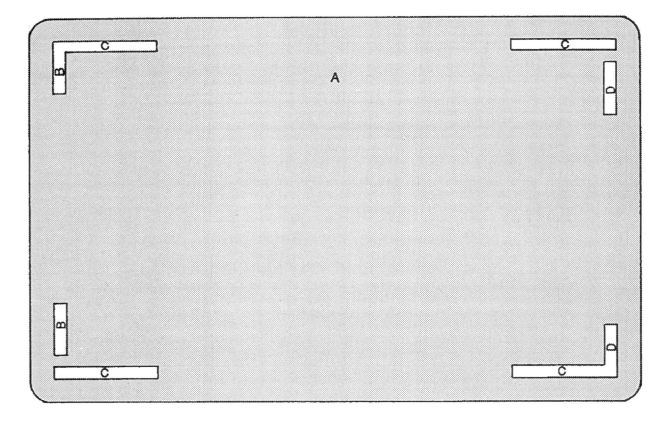

Small box full-size patterns.

MAKE 2

Fruit basket half-size patterns.

Fruit basket half-size patterns.

MAKE 2

98

Flower-vase holder half-size patterns. Enlarge them 200 percent for ⅛-inch-thick material.

The assembled flower-vase holder.

Making these three-dimensional tulips involves compound- and bevel-sawing techniques.

100

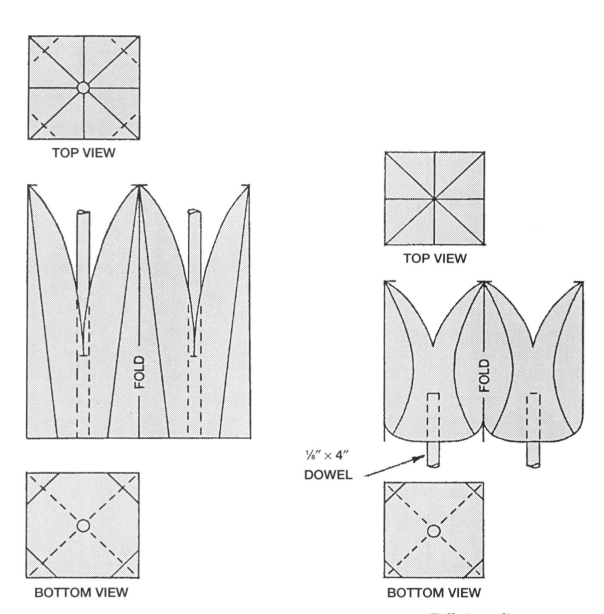

TOP VIEW

TOP VIEW

FOLD

FOLD

¹⁄₈″ × 4″
DOWEL

BOTTOM VIEW

BOTTOM VIEW

Full-size tulip patterns.

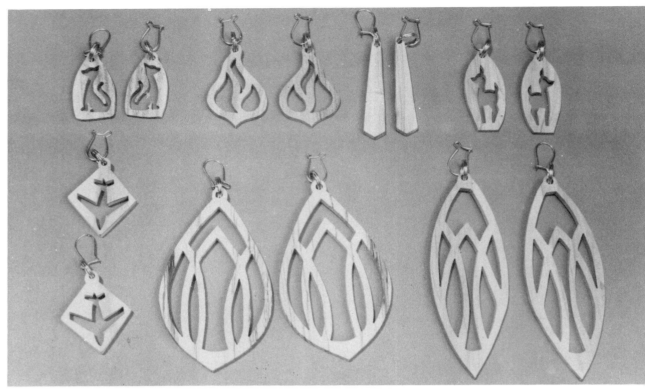

A variety of eardrop designs cut from thin solid woods.

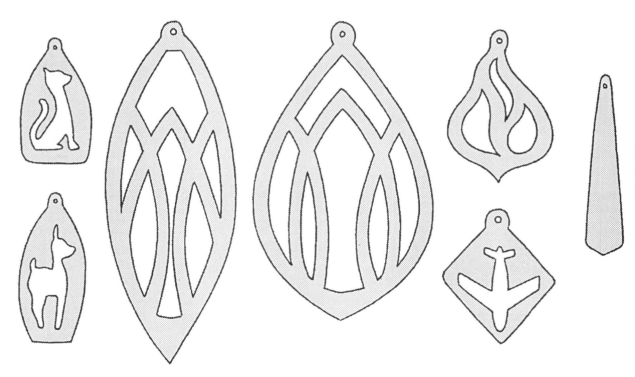

Eardrop full-size patterns.

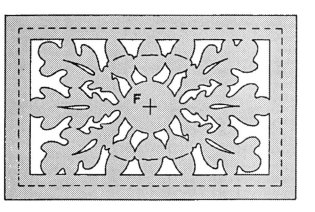

Small multiple-use box half-size patterns.

F

HALF-SIZE PATTERNS.
ENLARGE 200% FOR
⅛″ MATERIAL.

J, MAKE 2

G

NOTE: PARTS G, H, AND J ARE
PANELS TO LINE INTERIOR OF BOX
BEHIND PARTS F, B, AND D.

H, MAKE 2

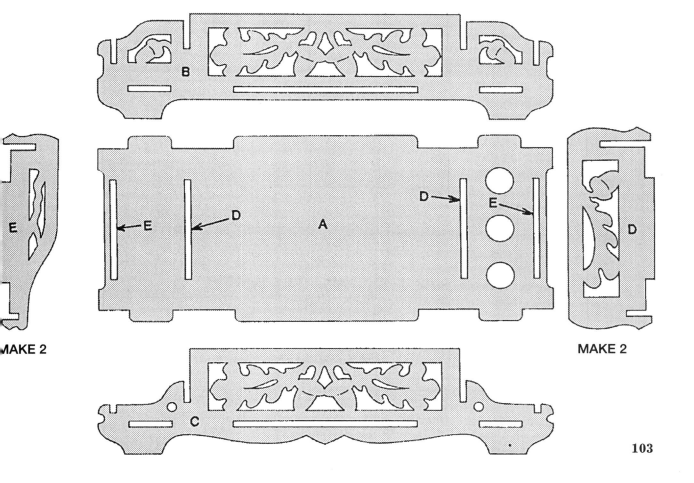

B

E

D

E

D

A

E

D

MAKE 2

MAKE 2

C

Multiple-use box complete and assembled.

This decorative carriage features slot-and-tab construction of ⅛-inch-thick plywood.

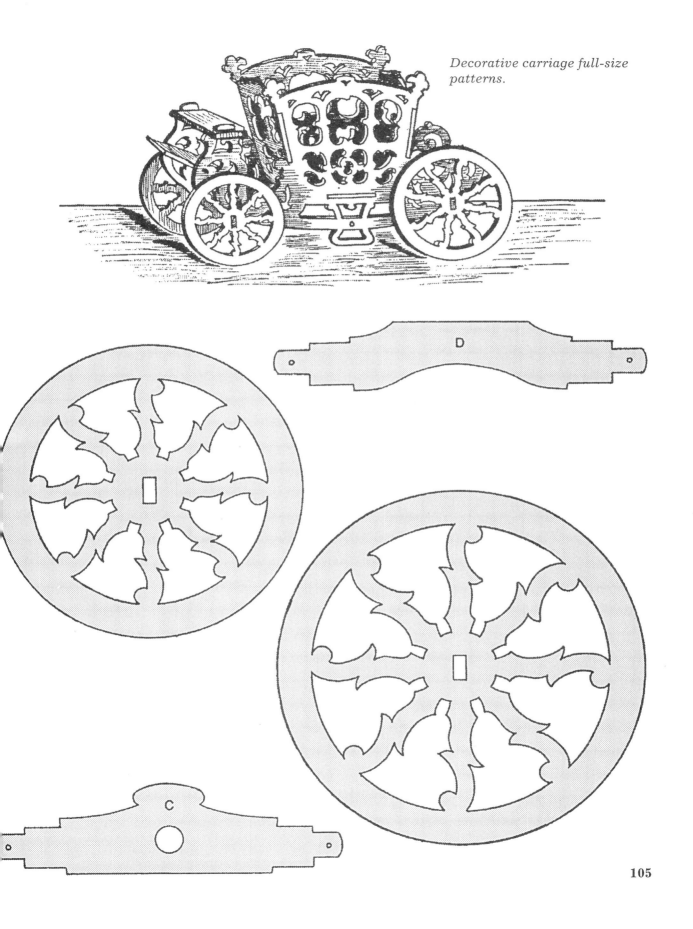

Decorative carriage full-size patterns.

D

C

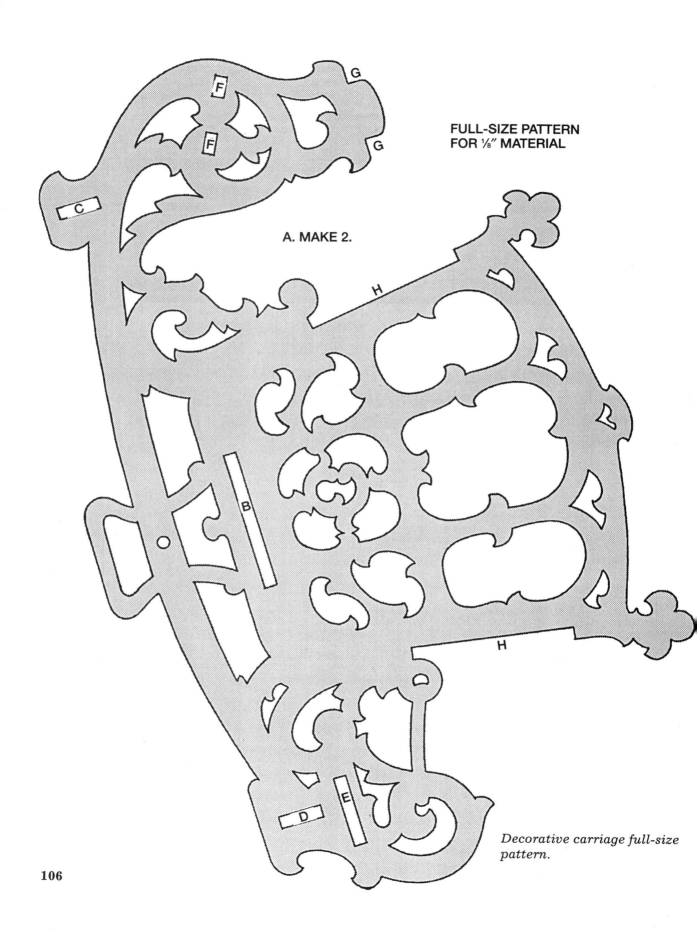

FULL-SIZE PATTERN
FOR ⅛" MATERIAL

A. MAKE 2.

Decorative carriage full-size pattern.

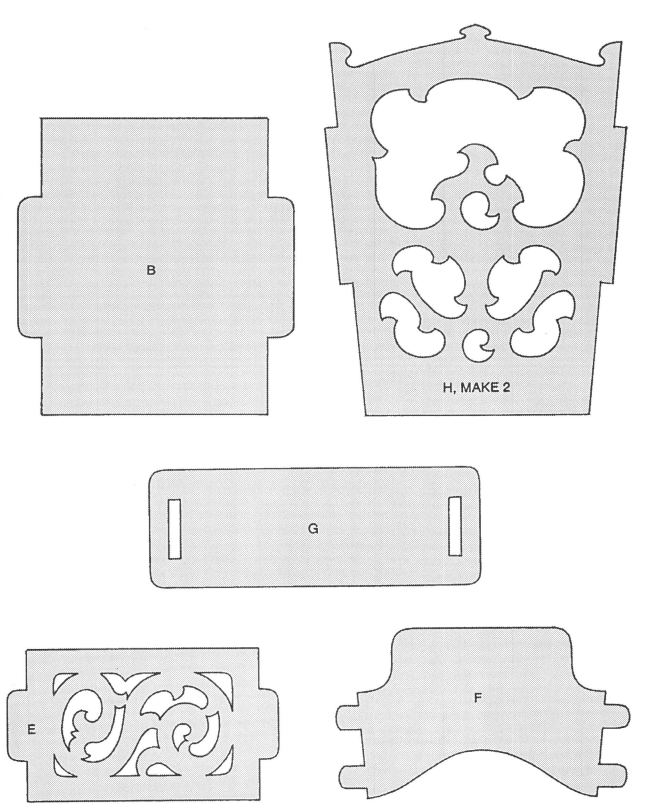

Decorative carriage full-size patterns.

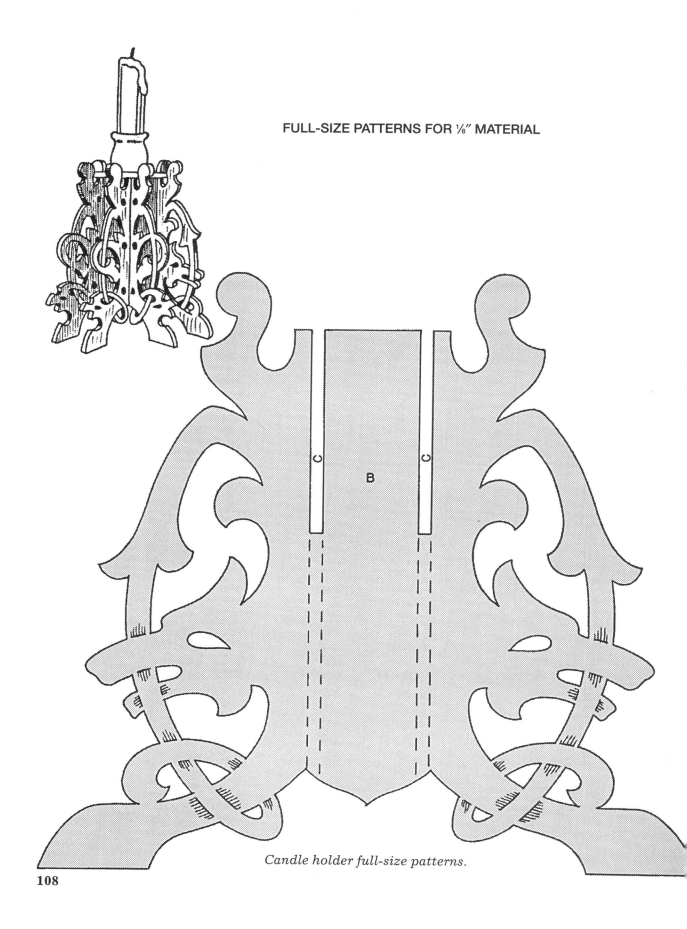

FULL-SIZE PATTERNS FOR ⅛″ MATERIAL

C C

B

Candle holder full-size patterns.

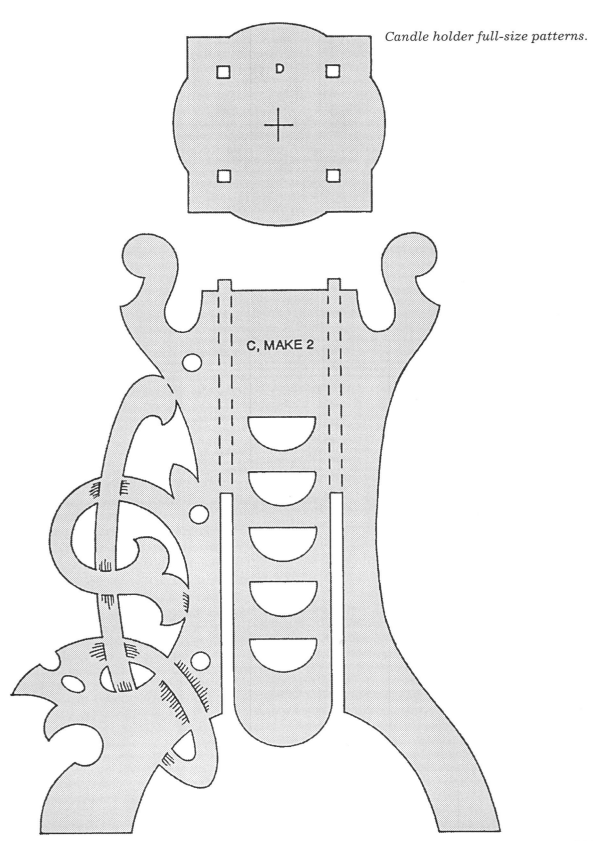

Candle holder full-size patterns.

D

C, MAKE 2

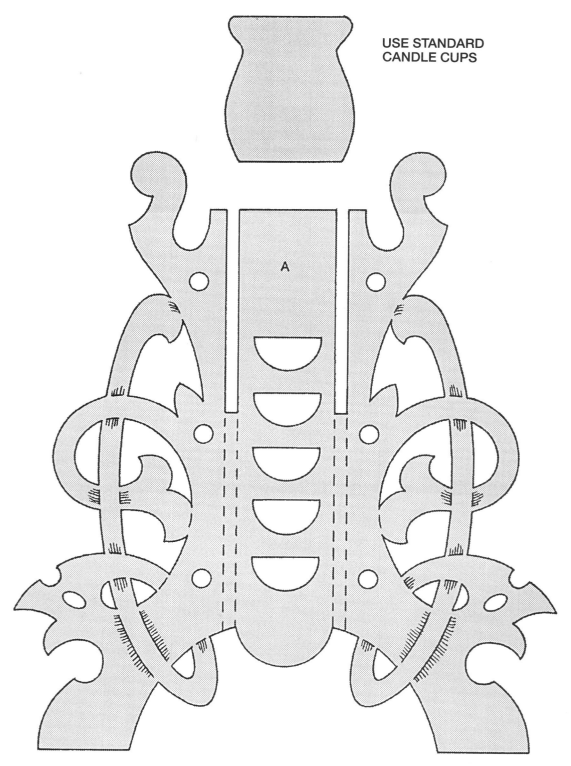

USE STANDARD
CANDLE CUPS

A

Candle holder full-size patterns.

Photo frame full-size patterns.

Photo frame full-size pattern.

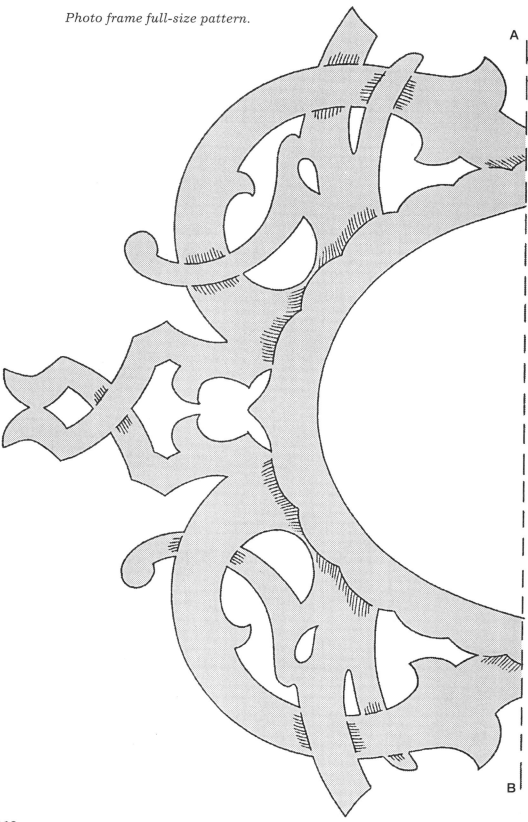

A

B

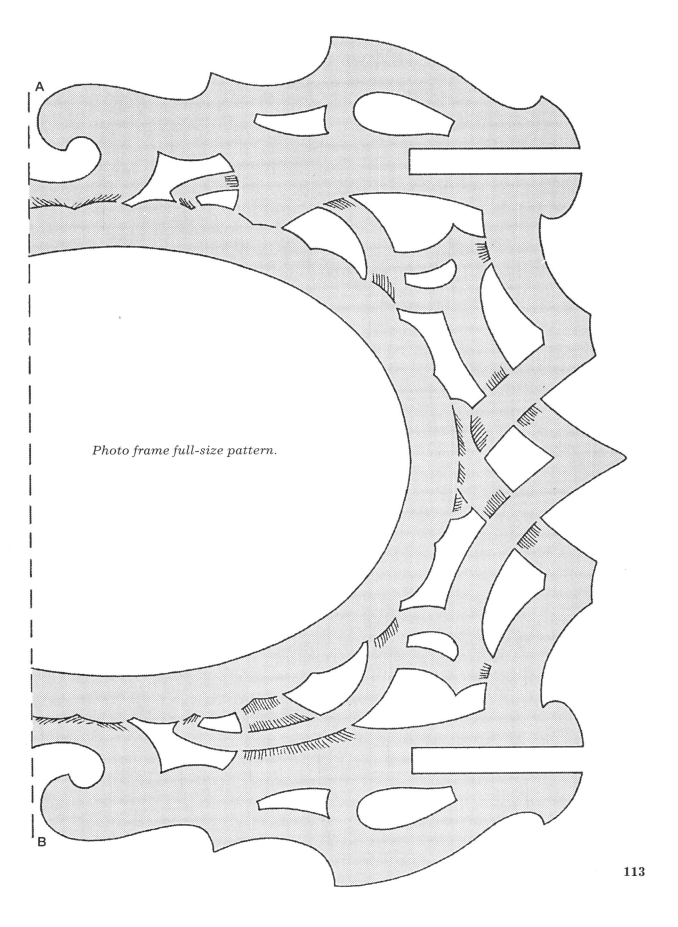

Photo frame full-size pattern.

A

B

113

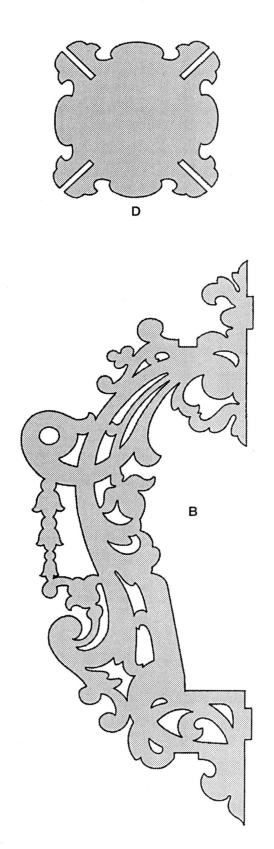

D

B

Hanging plant holder half-size patterns.

Hanging plant holder half-size patterns.

A

F   F

F

E

HALF-SIZE
PATTERNS.
ENLARGE 200%
FOR ⅛″
MATERIAL.

E

D

E   E

C

G, MAKE 2

F, MAKE 2

H, MAKE 2

D, MAKE 2

Full-size patterns for box with sliding lids.

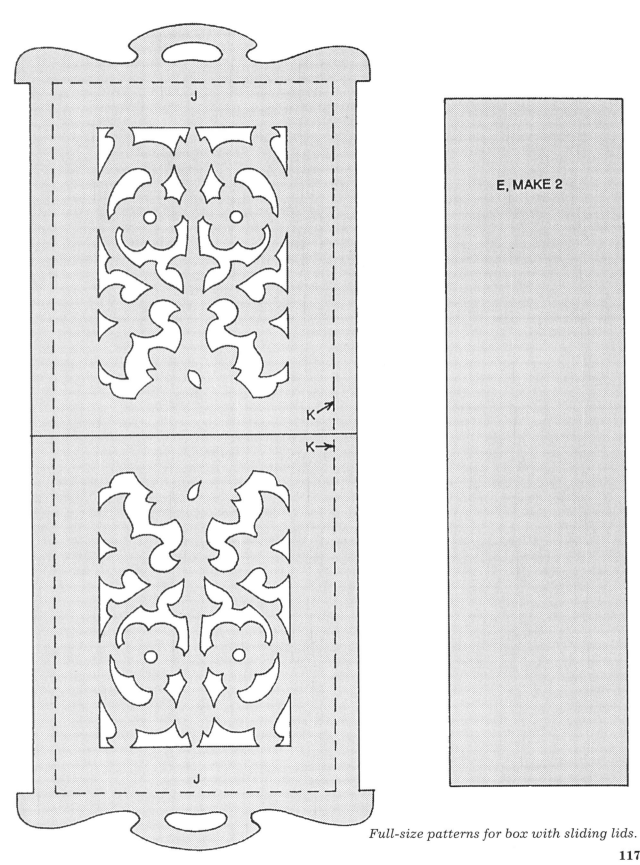

Full-size patterns for box with sliding lids.

117

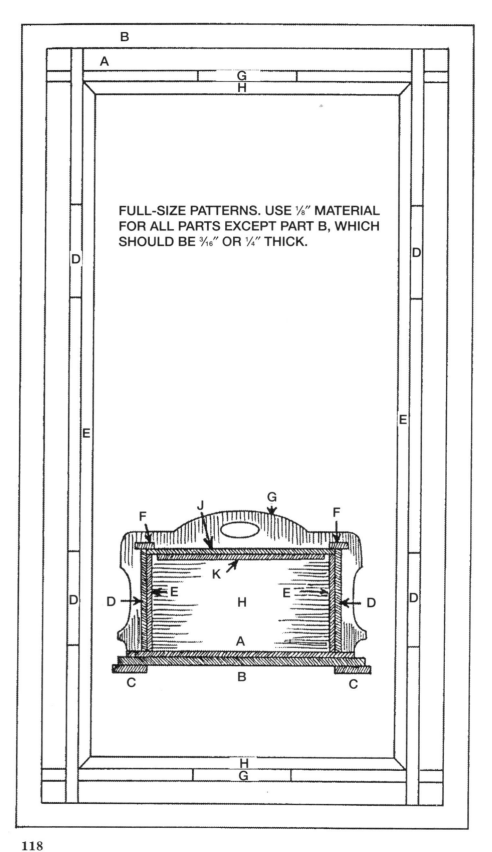

B

A

G
H

FULL-SIZE PATTERNS. USE ⅛″ MATERIAL
FOR ALL PARTS EXCEPT PART B, WHICH
SHOULD BE ³⁄₁₆″ OR ¼″ THICK.

D

D

E

E

J G

F F

K

D D E E D D

H

A

C B C

H
G

*Full-size patterns for box
with sliding lids.*

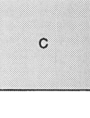

C

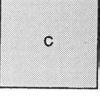

C

C

C

118

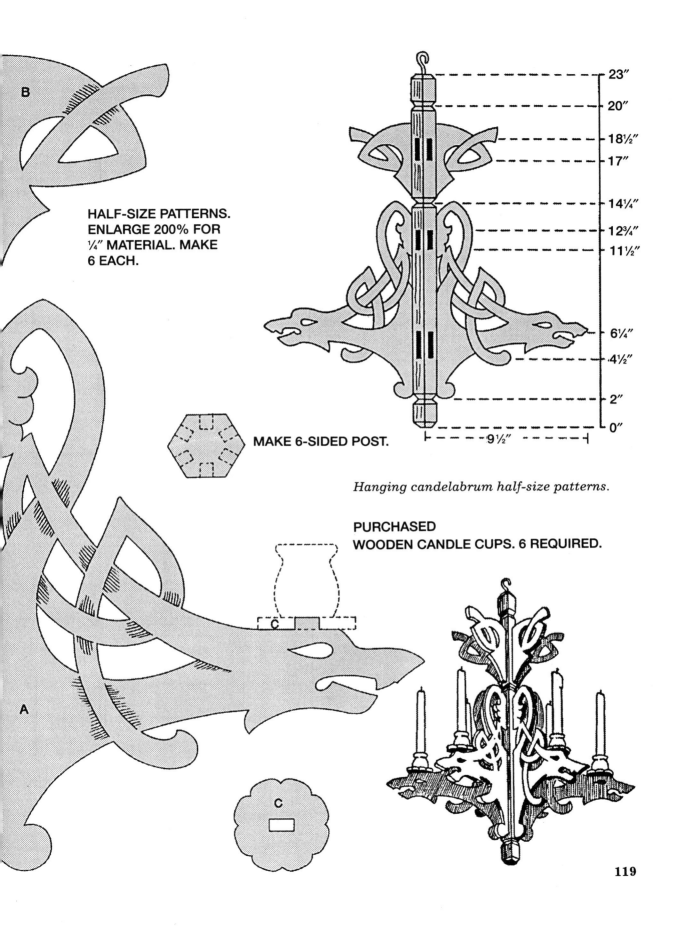

B

HALF-SIZE PATTERNS.
ENLARGE 200% FOR
¼" MATERIAL. MAKE
6 EACH.

MAKE 6-SIDED POST.

23"
20"
18½"
17"
14¼"
12¾"
11½"
6¼"
4½"
2"
0"

9½"

Hanging candelabrum half-size patterns.

PURCHASED
WOODEN CANDLE CUPS. 6 REQUIRED.

C

A

C

119

Mirror shelf half-size patterns.

HALF-SIZE PATTERNS. ENLARGE 200% FOR 1/4" MATERIAL.

A

Wall clock full-size pattern.

B

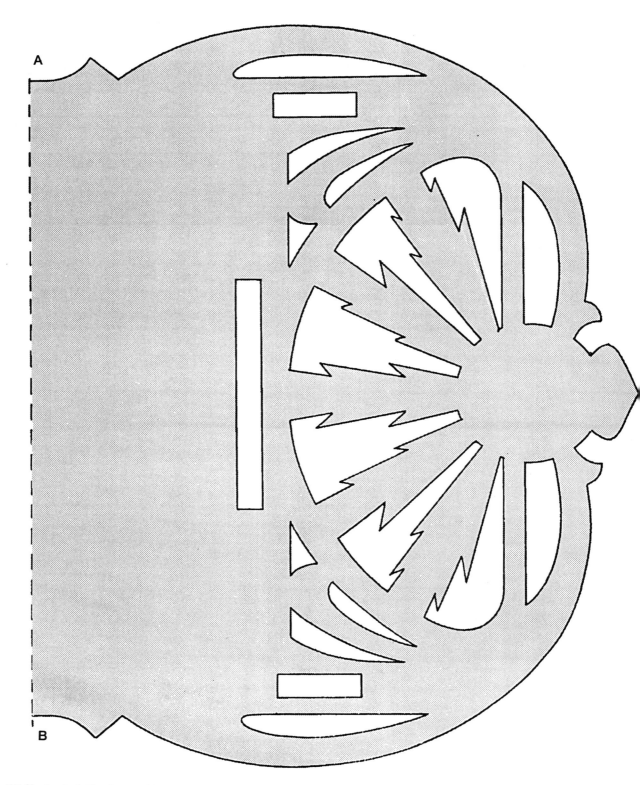

Wall clock full-size pattern.

122

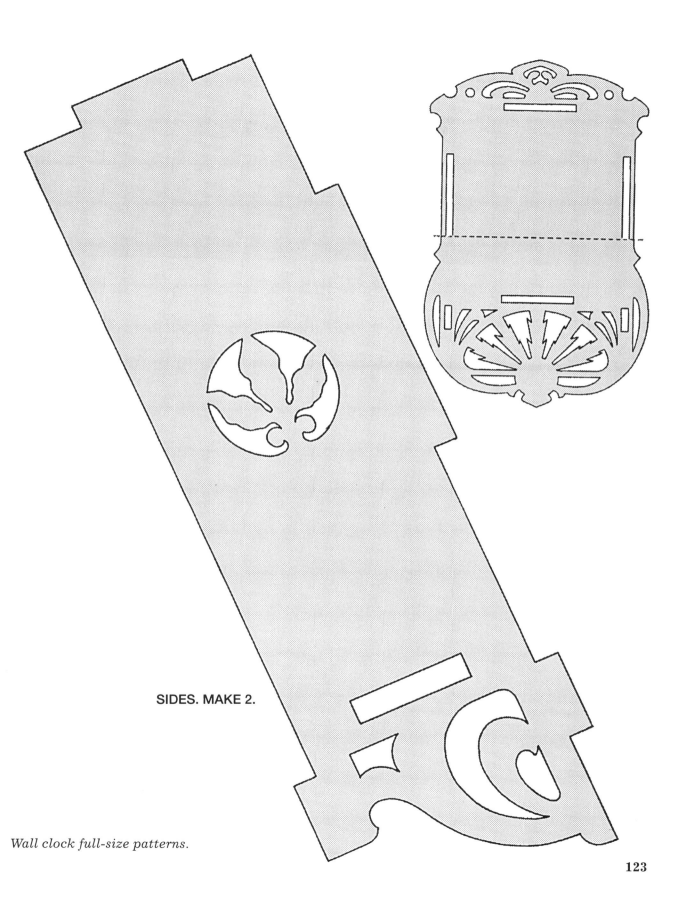

SIDES. MAKE 2.

Wall clock full-size patterns.

MAKE MOUNTING HOLE
SIZE AS REQ. FOR
CLOCK INSERTS UP TO
4" O.D. DIA.

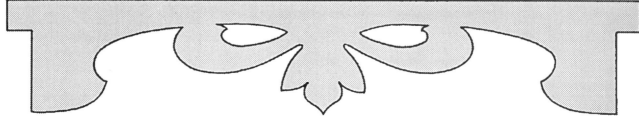

Wall clock full-size patterns.

124

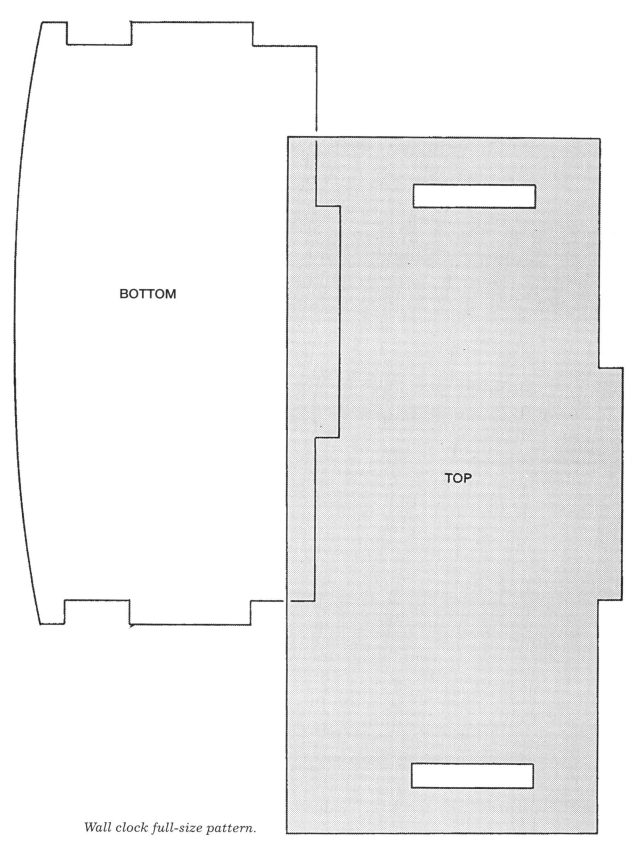

BOTTOM

TOP

Wall clock full-size pattern.

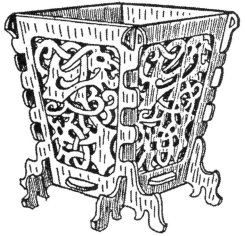

HALF-SIZE PATTERNS. ENLARGE 200% FOR ¼" MATERIAL.

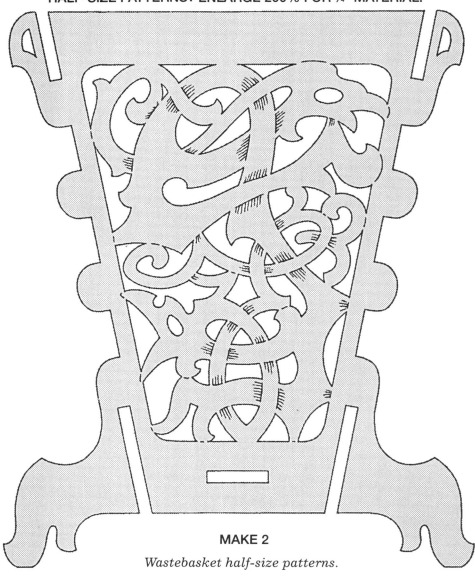

MAKE 2

Wastebasket half-size patterns.

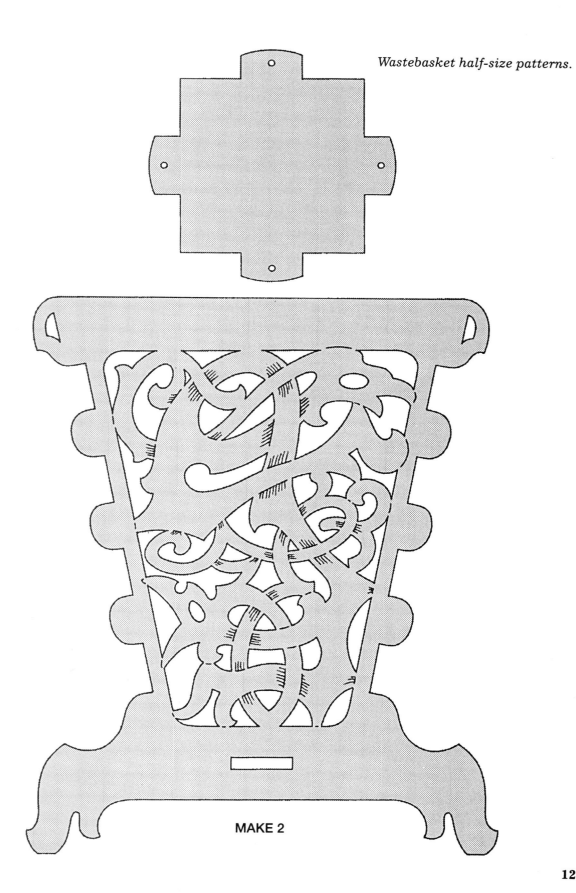

Wastebasket half-size patterns.

MAKE 2

This novel message-holder project, which can contain a special photo, advertisement, or message, will tempt inquisitive people.

The spring-like top, made by an endless squared spiral cut in plywood, reveals the contents inside when lifted.

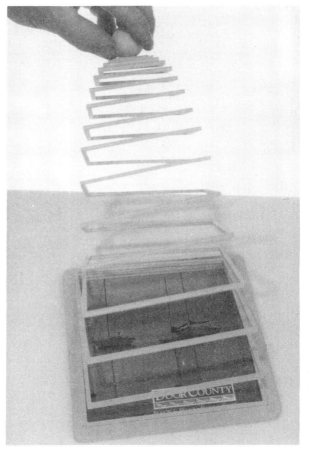

When the spring-like top is fully extended, the contents are completely visible.

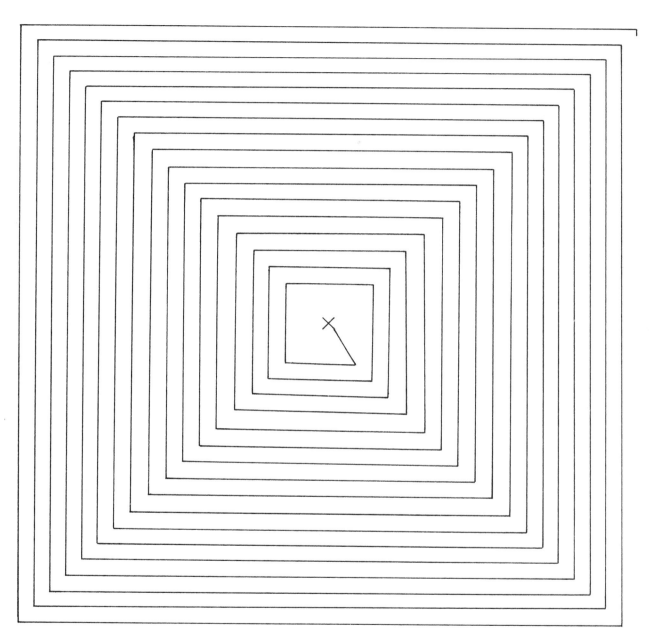

NOTE: CENTER CUTTING PATTERN ON
⅛″ × 7½″ **SQUARE PLYWOOD.**

Novelty message-holder pattern. This is the full-size cutting pattern for the top layer of two square pieces of plywood. The top is glued to the base only around the outer edges.

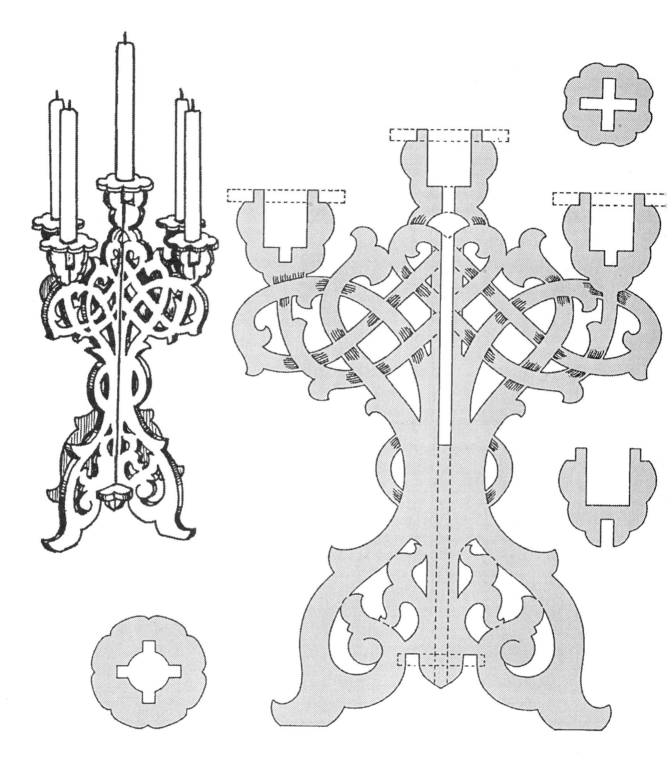

HALF-SIZE PATTERNS. ENLARGE 200% FOR ¼" MATERIAL.

Candelabrum half-size patterns.

130

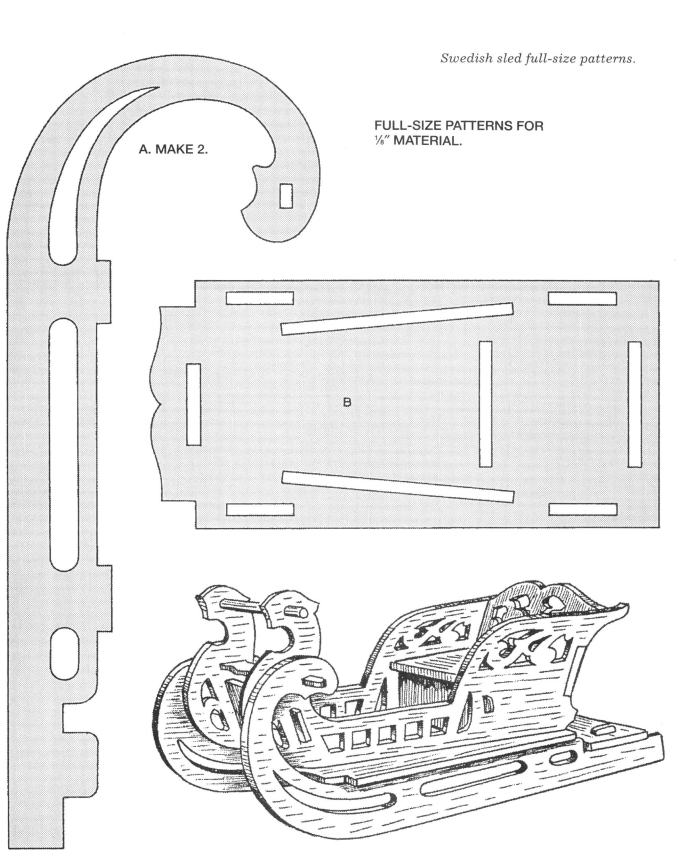

Swedish sled full-size patterns.

A. MAKE 2.

FULL-SIZE PATTERNS FOR
⅛″ MATERIAL.

B

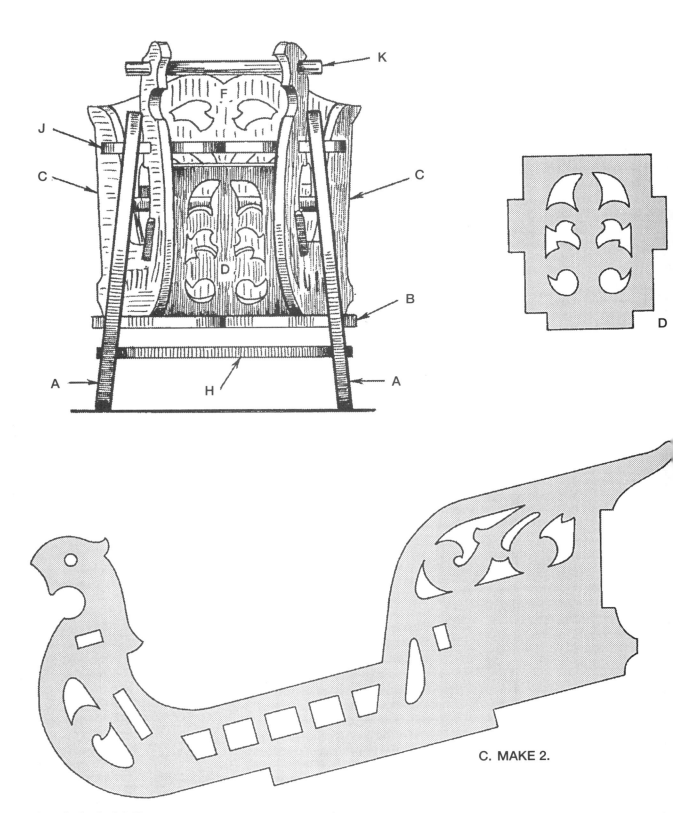

K

J

C

C

F

D

B

A

A

H

D

C. MAKE 2.

Swedish sled full-size patterns.

132

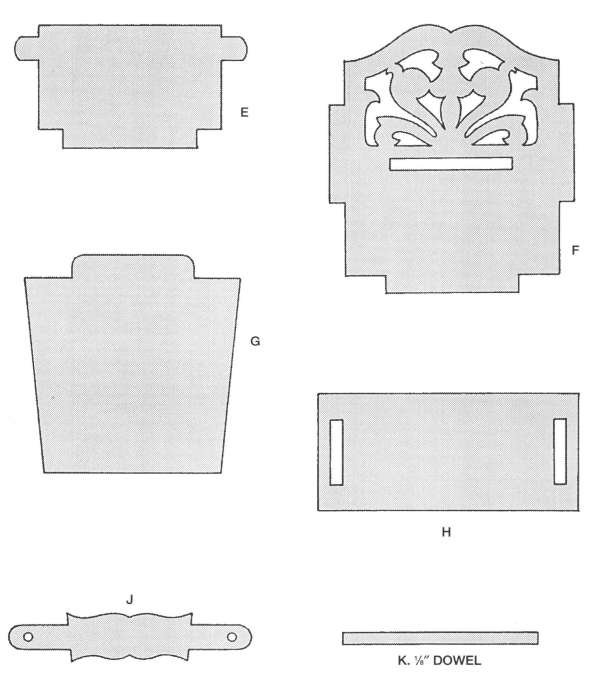

E

F

G

H

J

K. ⅛" DOWEL

Swedish sled full-size patterns.

133

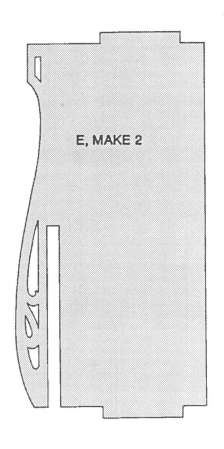

E, MAKE 2

HALF-SIZE PATTERNS. ENLARGE 200% FOR ¼″ MATERIAL. USE ¾″ MATERIAL FOR PART A, ½″ MATERIAL FOR PART C.

Mantel clock half-size patterns.

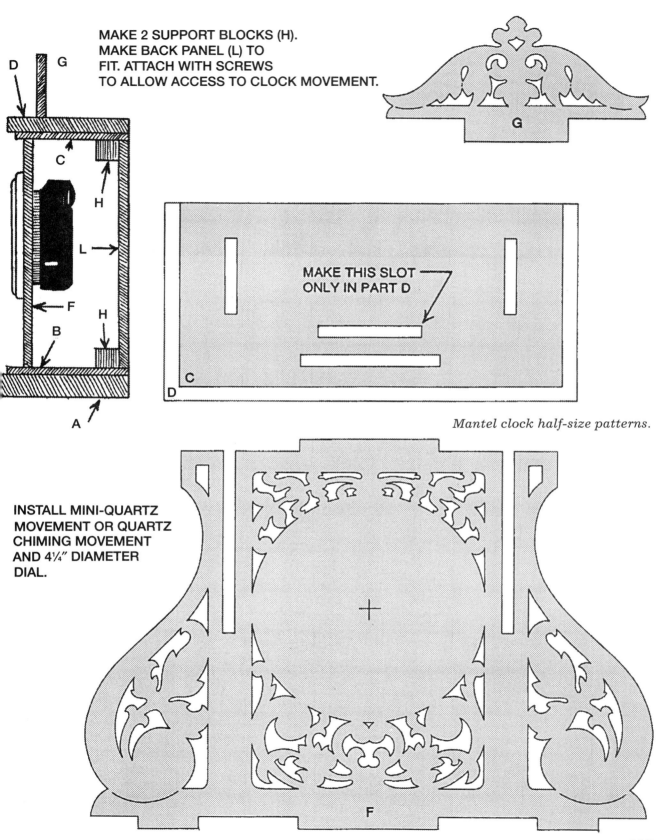

MAKE 2 SUPPORT BLOCKS (H).
MAKE BACK PANEL (L) TO
FIT. ATTACH WITH SCREWS
TO ALLOW ACCESS TO CLOCK MOVEMENT.

MAKE THIS SLOT
ONLY IN PART D

Mantel clock half-size patterns.

INSTALL MINI-QUARTZ
MOVEMENT OR QUARTZ
CHIMING MOVEMENT
AND 4¼" DIAMETER
DIAL.

135

Small trinket box full-size patterns.

**FULL-SIZE PATTERNS FOR
⅛″ MATERIAL**

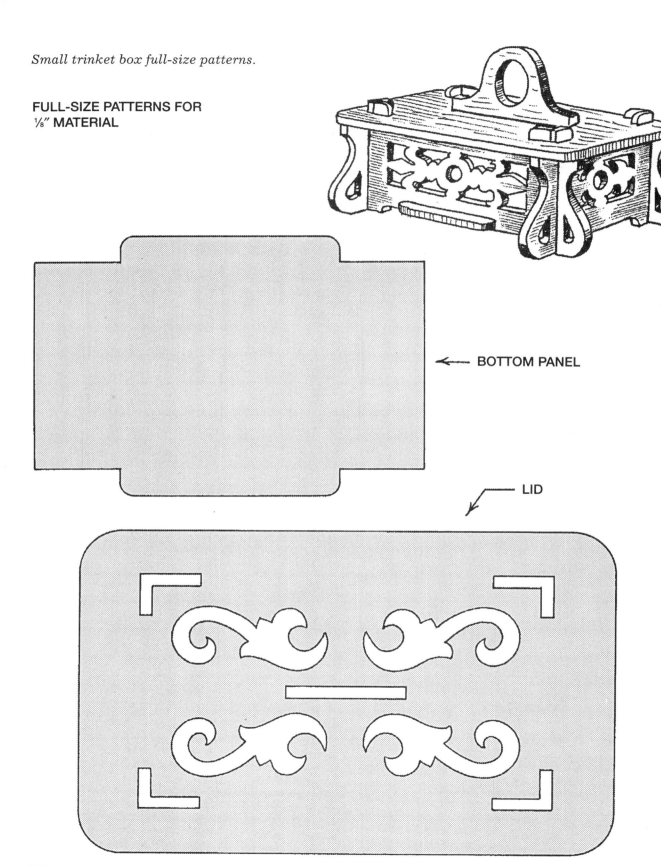

← BOTTOM PANEL

LID

FULL-SIZE PATTERNS FOR ⅛″ MATERIAL

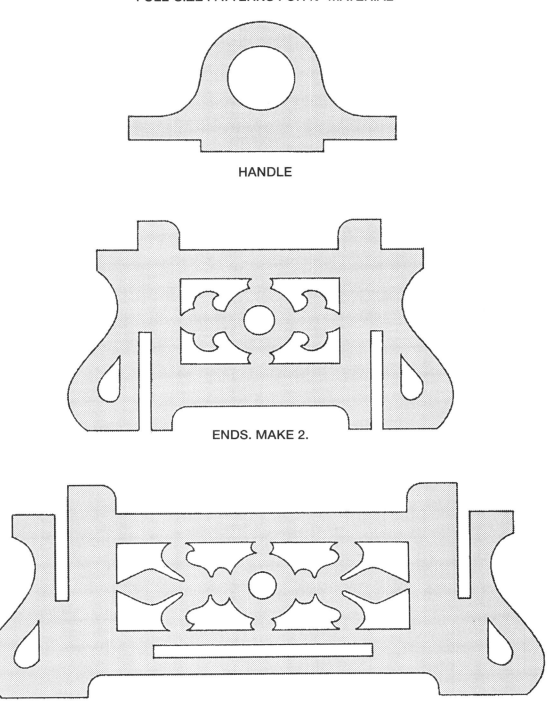

HANDLE

ENDS. MAKE 2.

FRONT & BACK. MAKE 2.

Small trinket box full-size patterns.

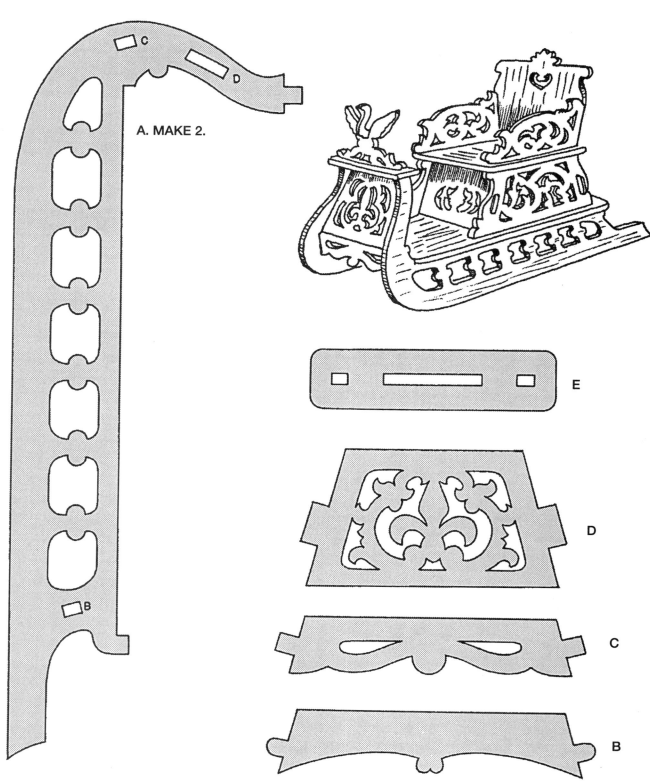

A. MAKE 2.

E

D

C

B

Dutch sleigh full-size patterns.

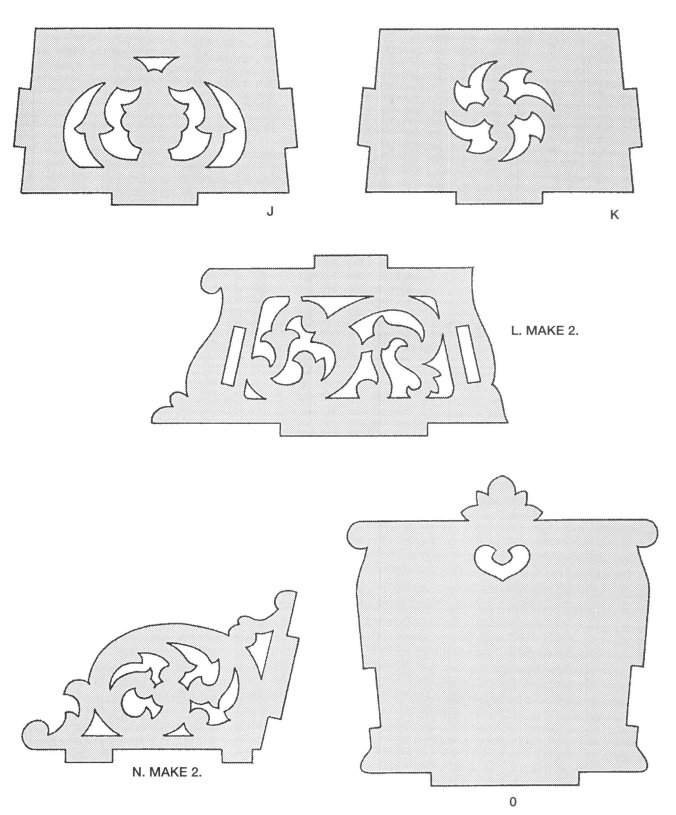

J

K

L. MAKE 2.

N. MAKE 2.

O

Dutch sleigh full-size patterns.

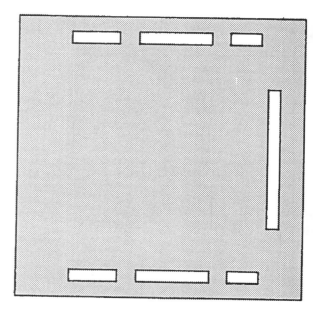

M

H

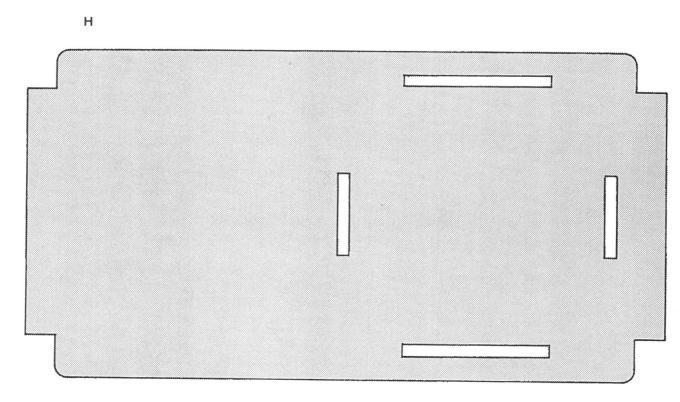

Dutch sleigh full-size patterns.

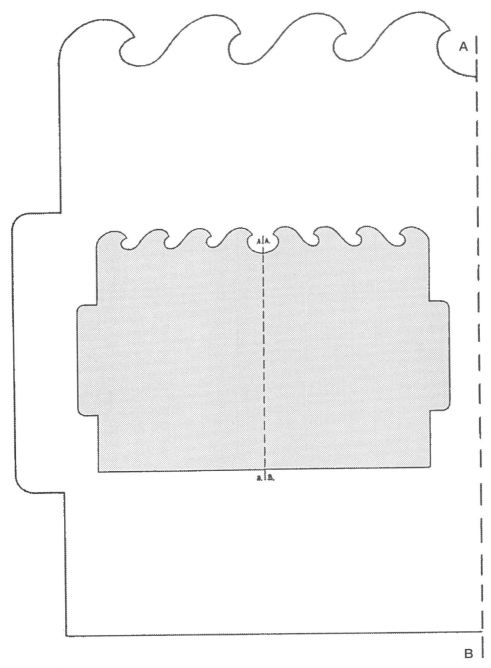

A

B

Book rack full-size pattern.

A

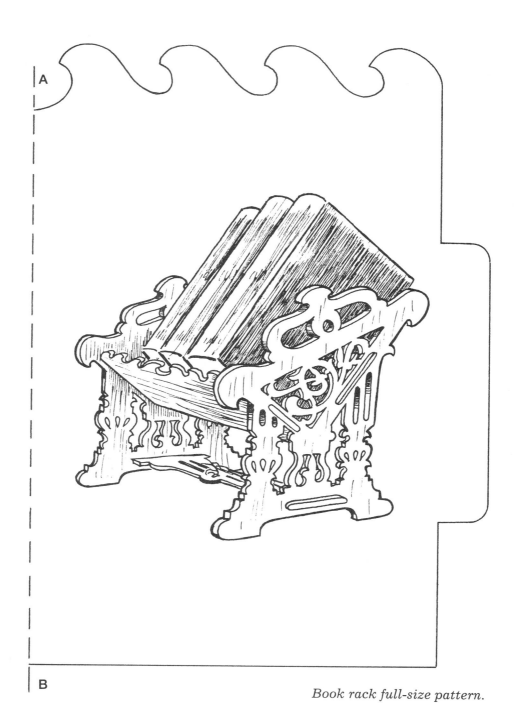

B

Book rack full-size pattern.

142

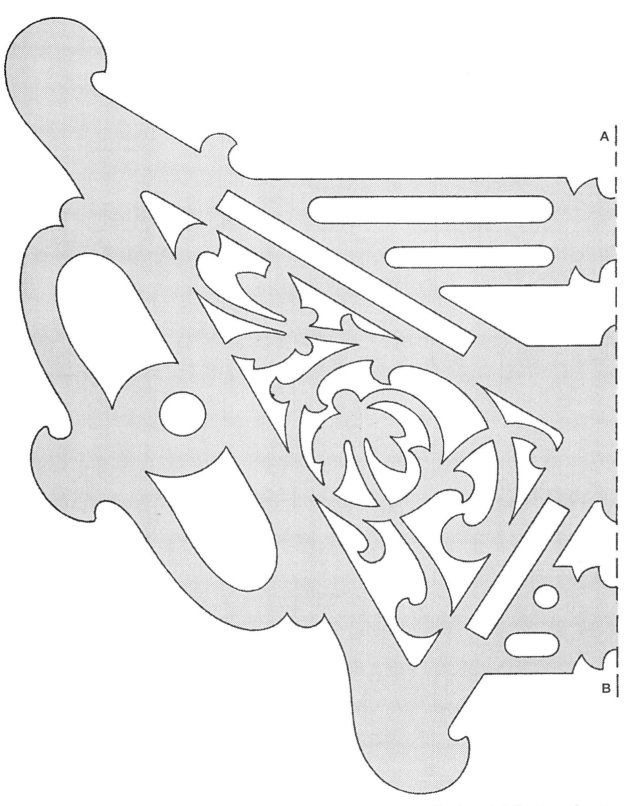

A

B

Book rack full-size end pattern.

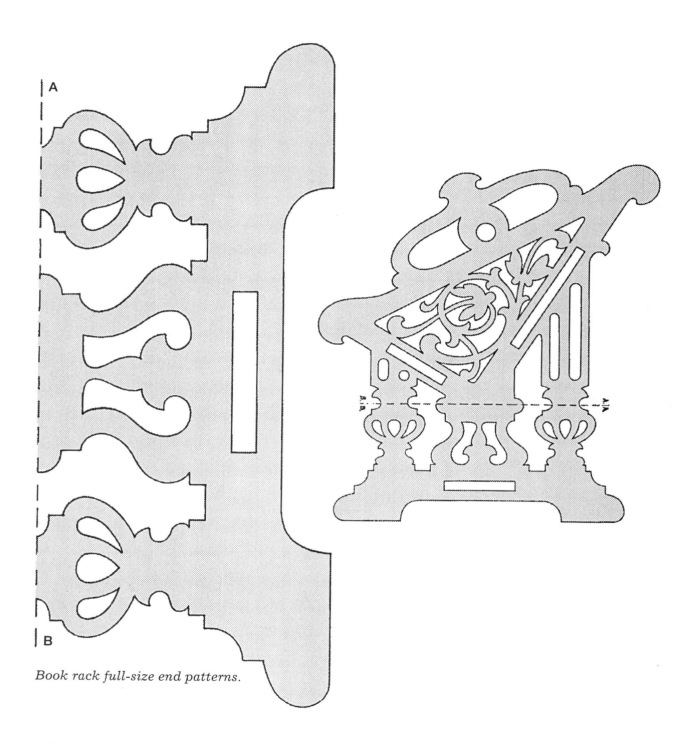

A

B

Book rack full-size end patterns.

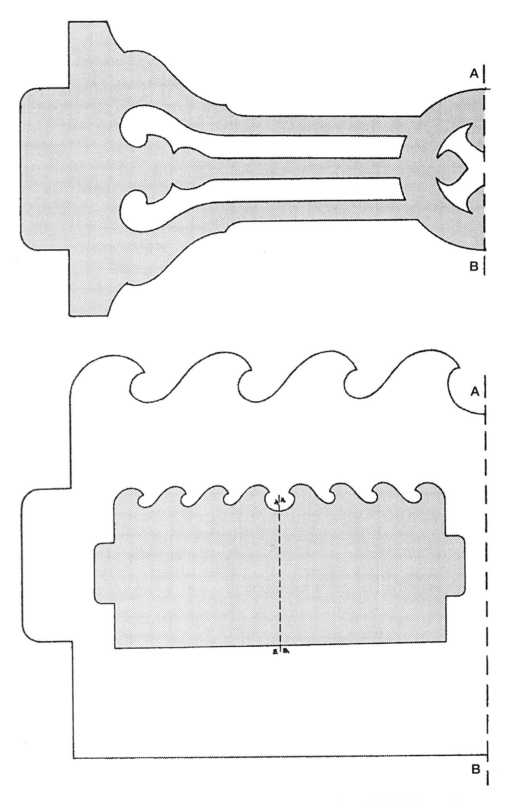

A

B

A

A

B

Book rack full-size patterns.

145

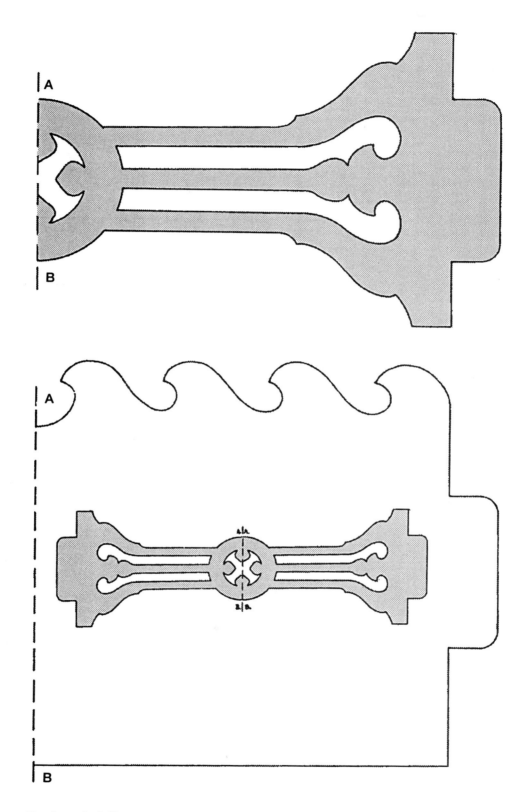

Book rack full-size patterns.

146

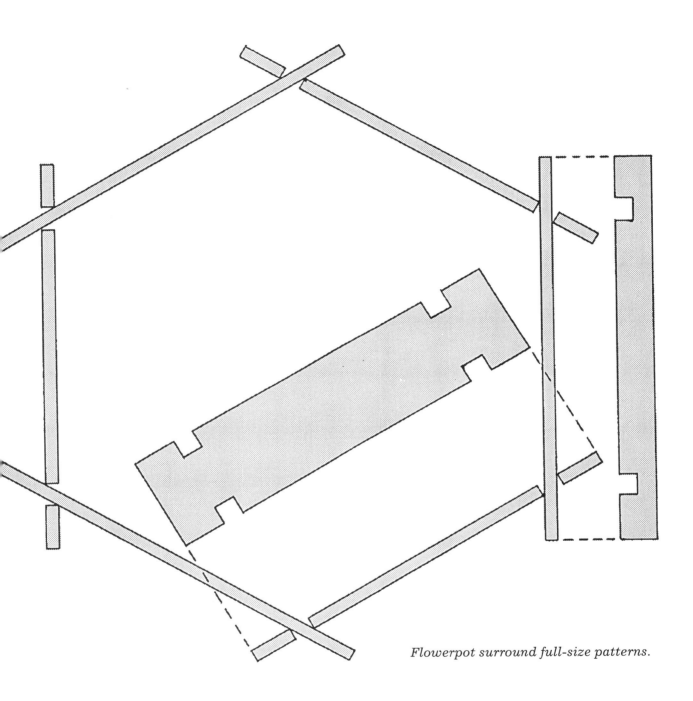

Flowerpot surround full-size patterns.

147

This hexagon flowerpot surround can be made to any size. All parts are held together by the outward pressure of each piece within slots cut to a specific width.

Swedish candle holder.

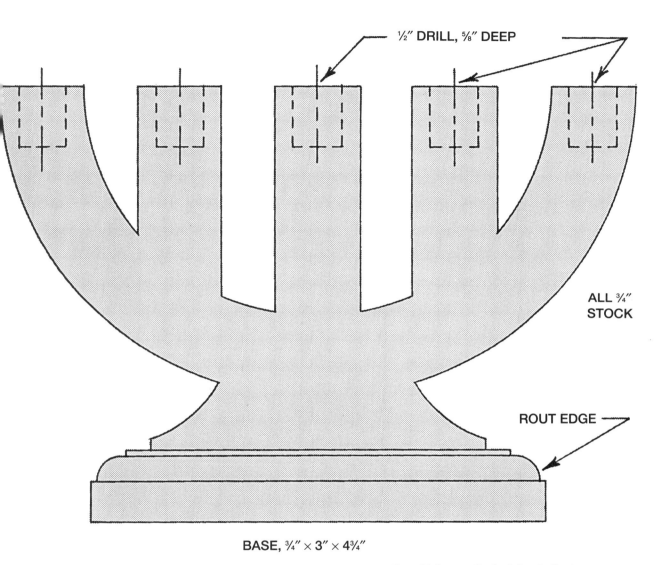

½″ DRILL, ⅝″ DEEP

ALL ¾″
STOCK

ROUT EDGE →

BASE, ¾″ × 3″ × 4¾″

Swedish candle holder full-size pattern.

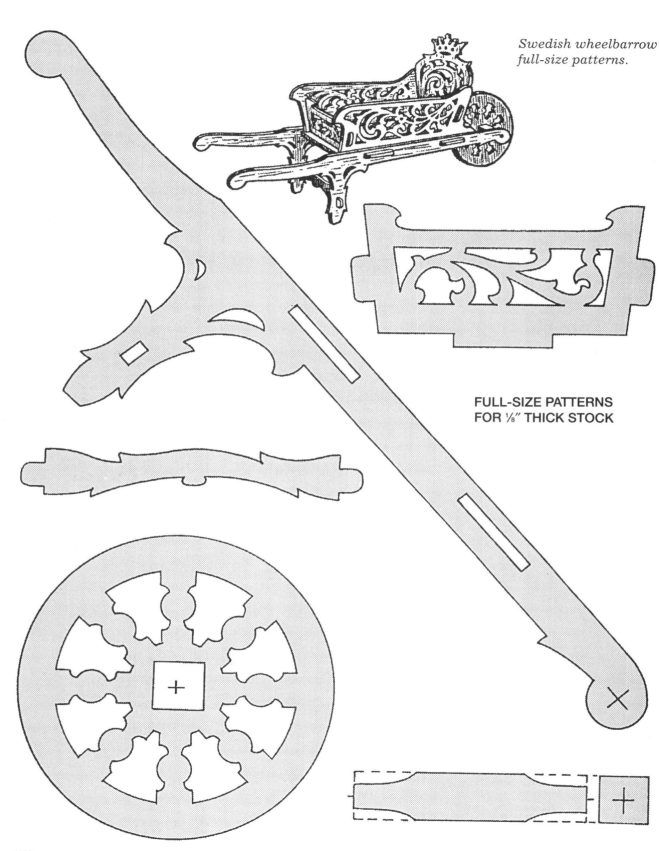

Swedish wheelbarrow full-size patterns.

**FULL-SIZE PATTERNS
FOR ⅛″ THICK STOCK**

150

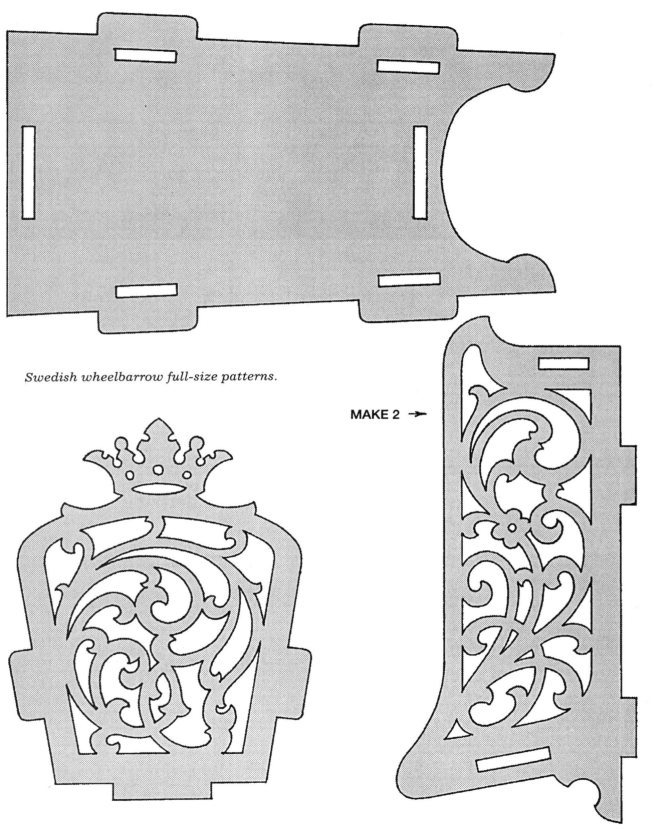

Swedish wheelbarrow full-size patterns.

MAKE 2 ➡

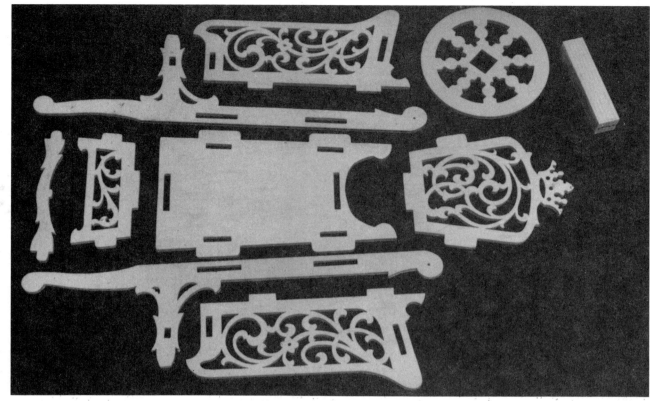

All of the parts for the Swedish wheelbarrow.

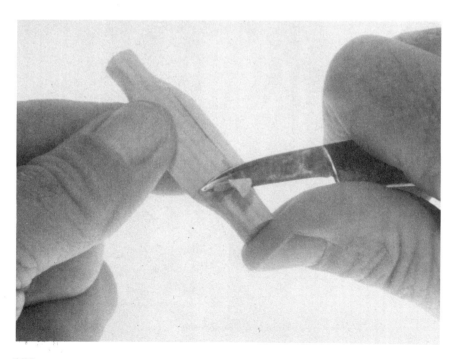

Carve the ends of the axle as shown.

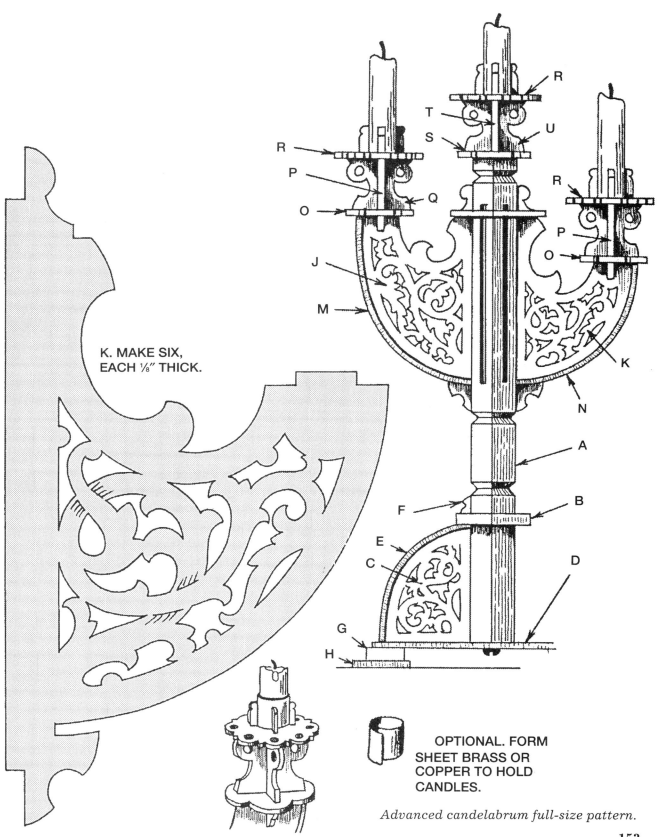

K. MAKE SIX,
EACH ⅛″ THICK.

OPTIONAL. FORM
SHEET BRASS OR
COPPER TO HOLD
CANDLES.

Advanced candelabrum full-size pattern.

153

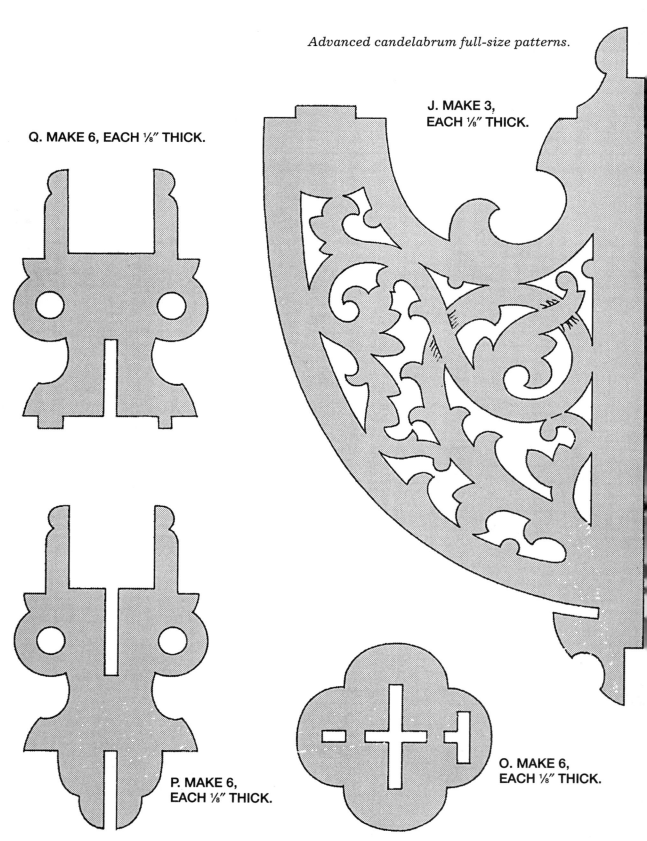

Advanced candelabrum full-size patterns.

J. MAKE 3,
EACH ⅛″ THICK.

Q. MAKE 6, EACH ⅛″ THICK.

P. MAKE 6,
EACH ⅛″ THICK.

O. MAKE 6,
EACH ⅛″ THICK.

154

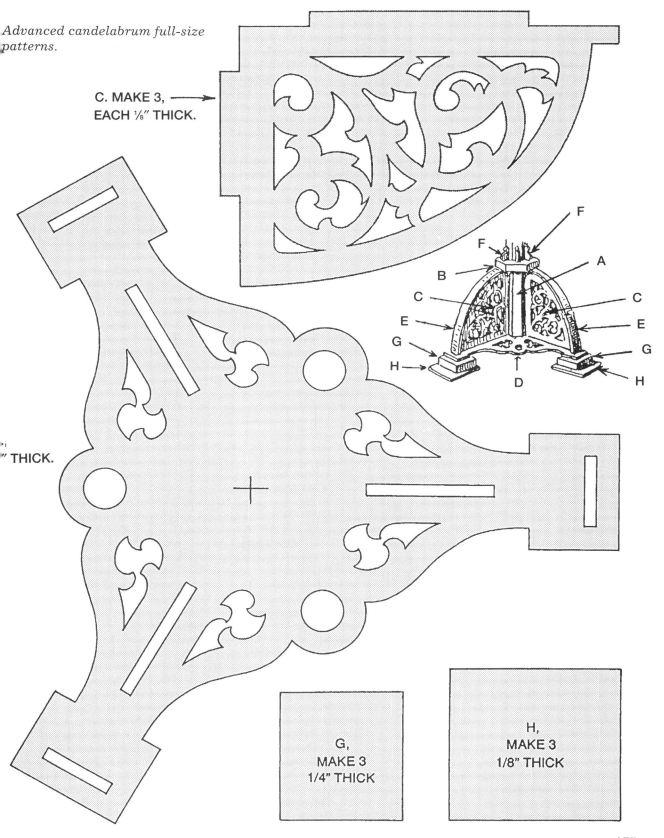

Advanced candelabrum full-size patterns.

C. MAKE 3,
EACH ⅛″ THICK.

″ THICK.

F

F

B

C

A

C

E

E

G

G

H

H

D

G,
MAKE 3
1/4" THICK

H,
MAKE 3
1/8" THICK

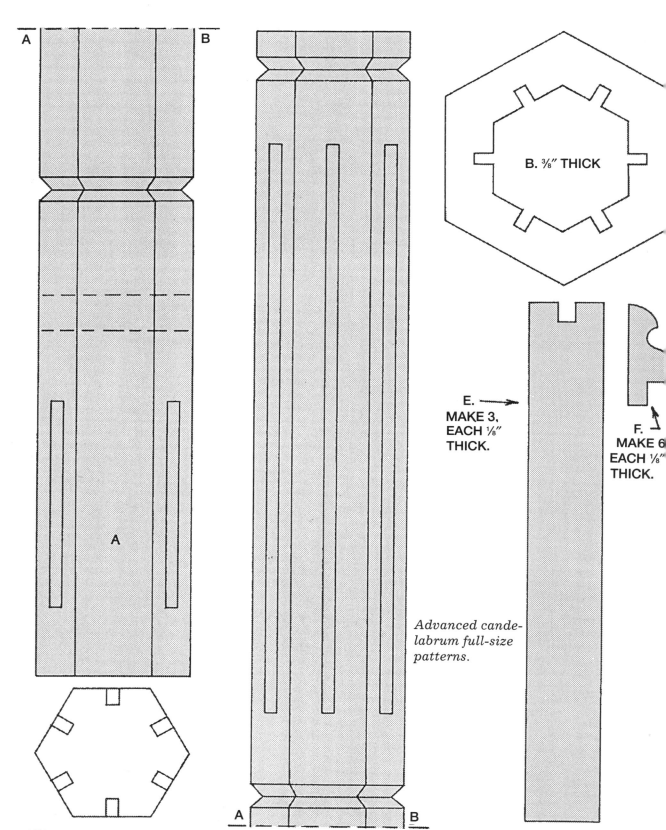

A

B

B. ⅜″ THICK

E. →
MAKE 3,
EACH ⅛″
THICK.

F.
MAKE 6
EACH ⅛″
THICK.

A

A   B

*Advanced cande-
labrum full-size
patterns.*

156

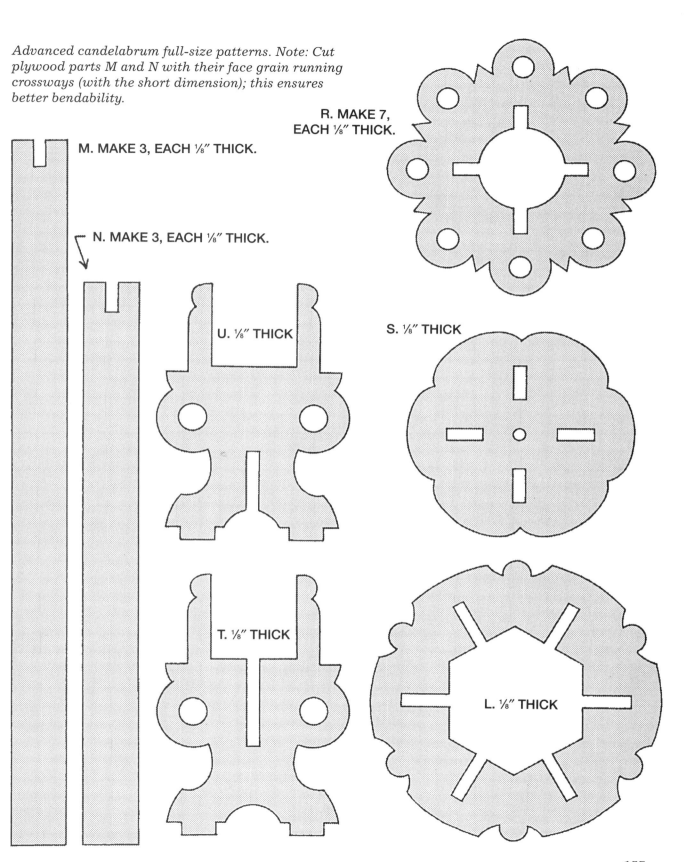

Advanced candelabrum full-size patterns. Note: Cut plywood parts M and N with their face grain running crossways (with the short dimension); this ensures better bendability.

M. MAKE 3, EACH ⅛″ THICK.

N. MAKE 3, EACH ⅛″ THICK.

R. MAKE 7, EACH ⅛″ THICK.

U. ⅛″ THICK

S. ⅛″ THICK

T. ⅛″ THICK

L. ⅛″ THICK

**HALF-SIZE PATTERN.
ENLARGE 200%.**

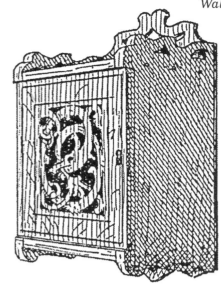

**DOOR. MAKE FROM
½" THICK MATERIAL.**

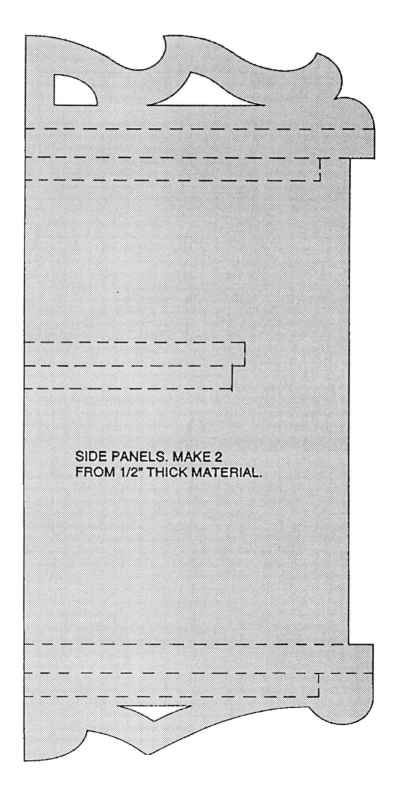

SIDE PANELS. MAKE 2
FROM 1/2" THICK MATERIAL.

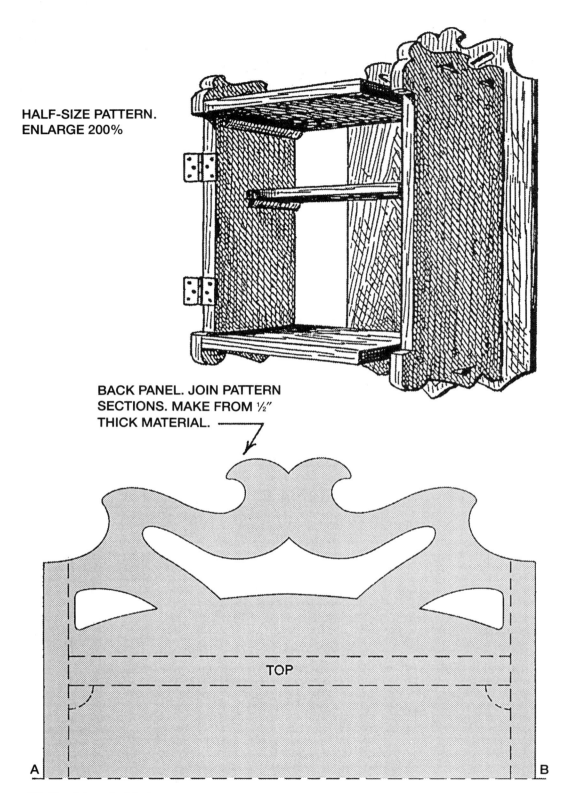

HALF-SIZE PATTERN.
ENLARGE 200%

BACK PANEL. JOIN PATTERN
SECTIONS. MAKE FROM ½"
THICK MATERIAL.

TOP

A

B

Wall cabinet half-size pattern.

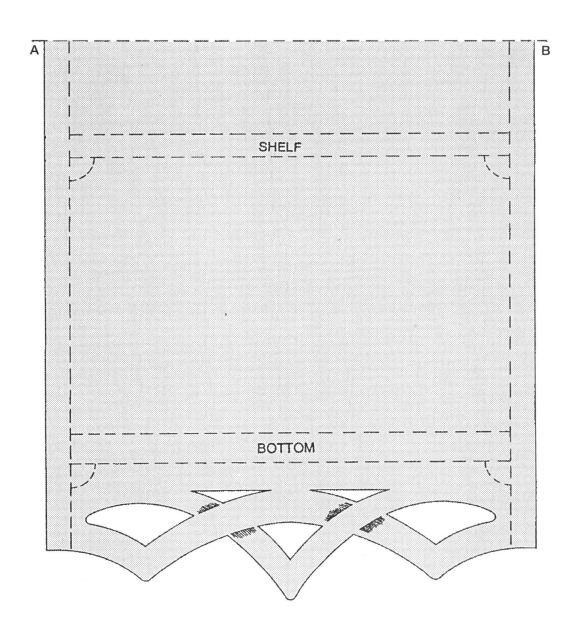

MAKE TOP & BOTTOM FROM ⅝″ THICK MATERIAL. MAKE
SHELF FROM ½″ THICK MATERIAL. USE ½″ × ½″ QUARTER-
ROUND FOR SUPPORTS.

Wall cabinet half-size pattern.

FULL-SIZE PATTERNS FOR ¼″ THICK MATERIAL.

BEVEL ENDS OF PART D.

EDGE VIEW OF D

Decorative box full-size patterns.

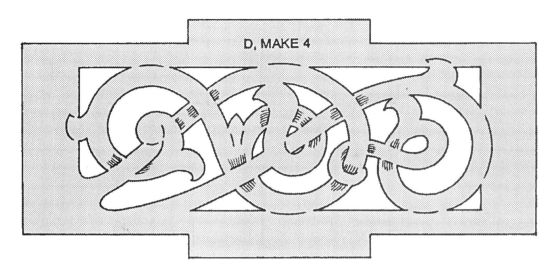

D, MAKE 4

Decorative box full-size patterns.

E

F

F

F

F

163

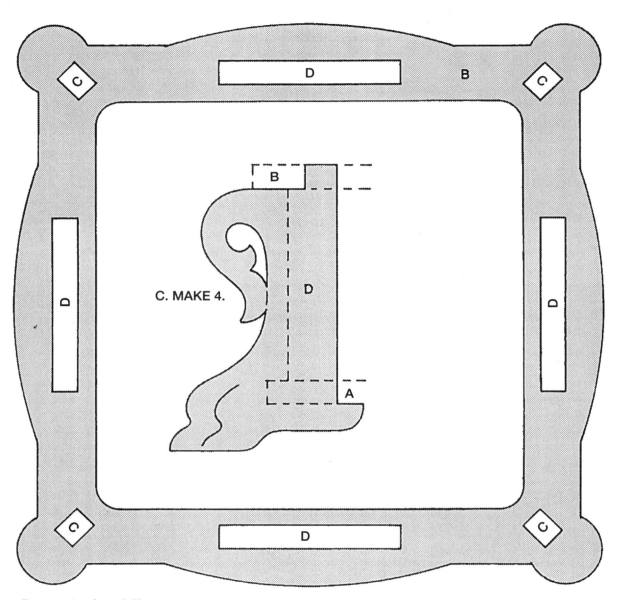

Decorative box full-size patterns.

164

F, MAKE 2

Decorative box full-size patterns.

G

E

G

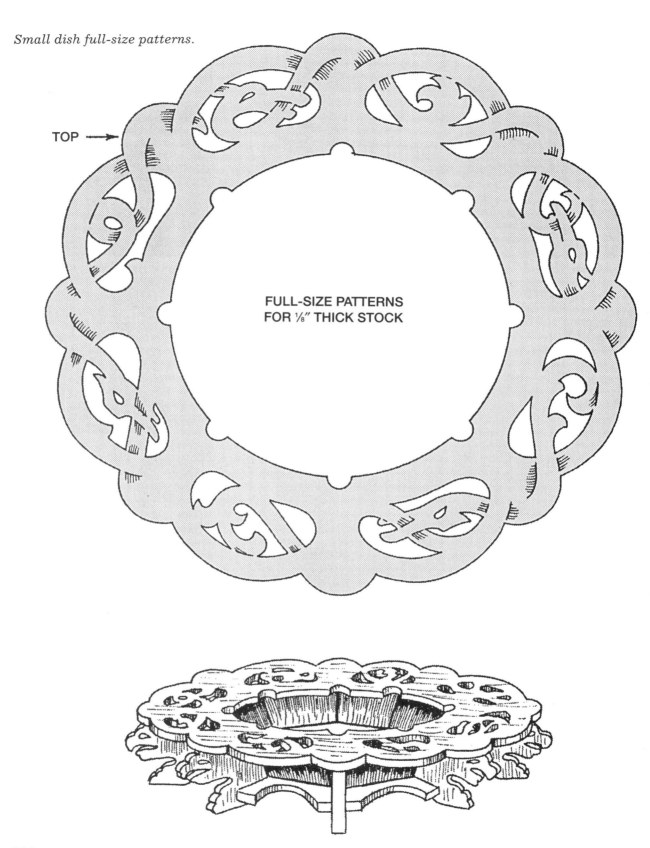

Small dish full-size patterns.

TOP →

FULL-SIZE PATTERNS
FOR ⅛″ THICK STOCK

TOP

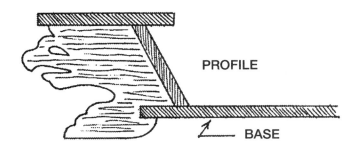

PROFILE

BASE

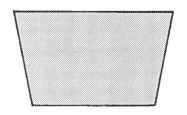

SIDES - MAKE 8.

BEVEL EDGES TO FIT.

LEGS. MAKE 8.

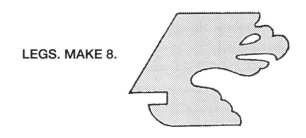

BASE →

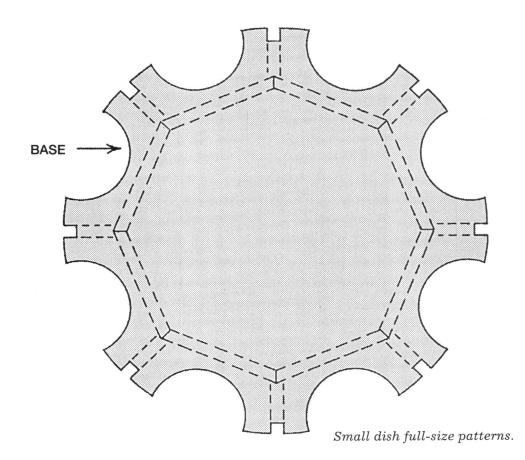

Small dish full-size patterns.

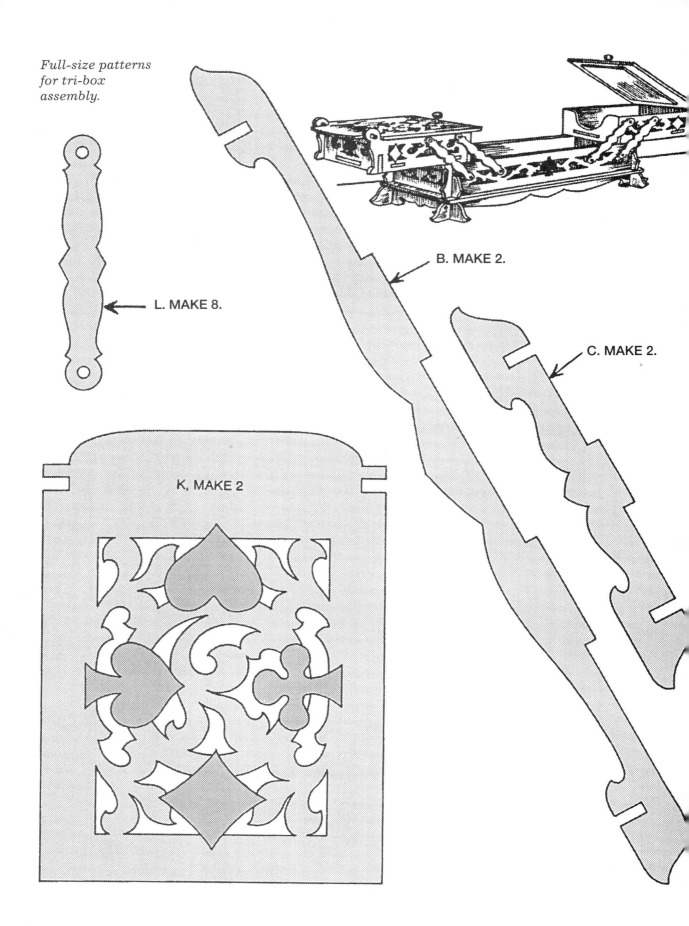

Full-size patterns for tri-box assembly.

L. MAKE 8.

B. MAKE 2.

C. MAKE 2.

K, MAKE 2

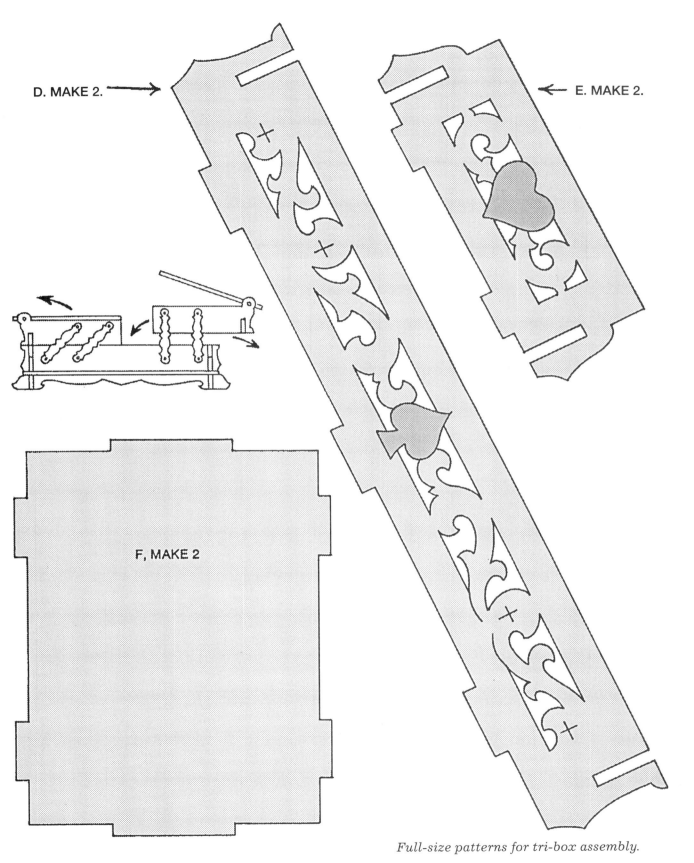

D. MAKE 2.

E. MAKE 2.

F, MAKE 2

Full-size patterns for tri-box assembly.

169

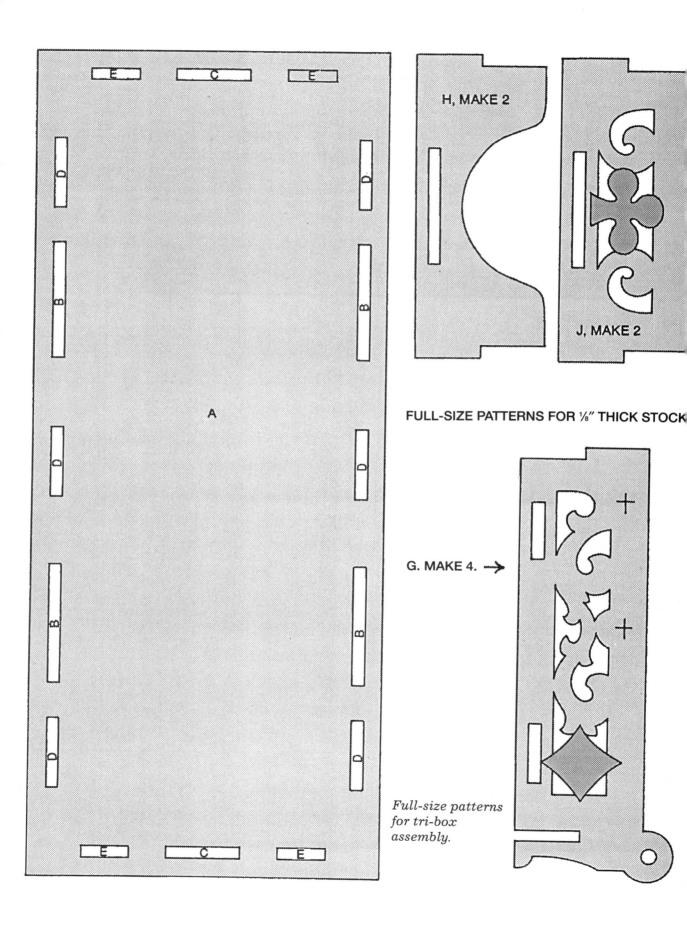

E C E

D D

B B

D D

A

B B

D D

E C E

H, MAKE 2

J, MAKE 2

FULL-SIZE PATTERNS FOR ⅛″ THICK STOCK

G. MAKE 4. →

*Full-size patterns
for tri-box
assembly.*

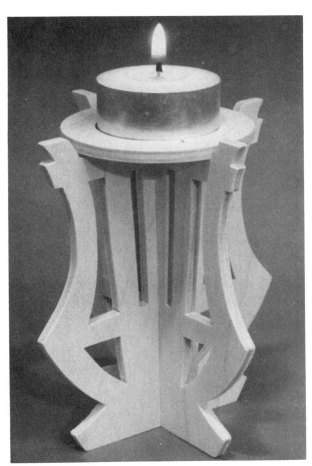

Decorative warming-candle holder. This nifty project is made from just three pieces of ⅛-inch-thick plywood.

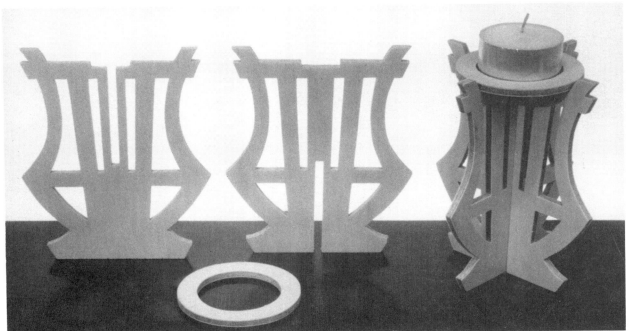

The parts of the warming-candle holder at left, and the assembled project at right.

Full-size patterns for decorative warming-candle holder.

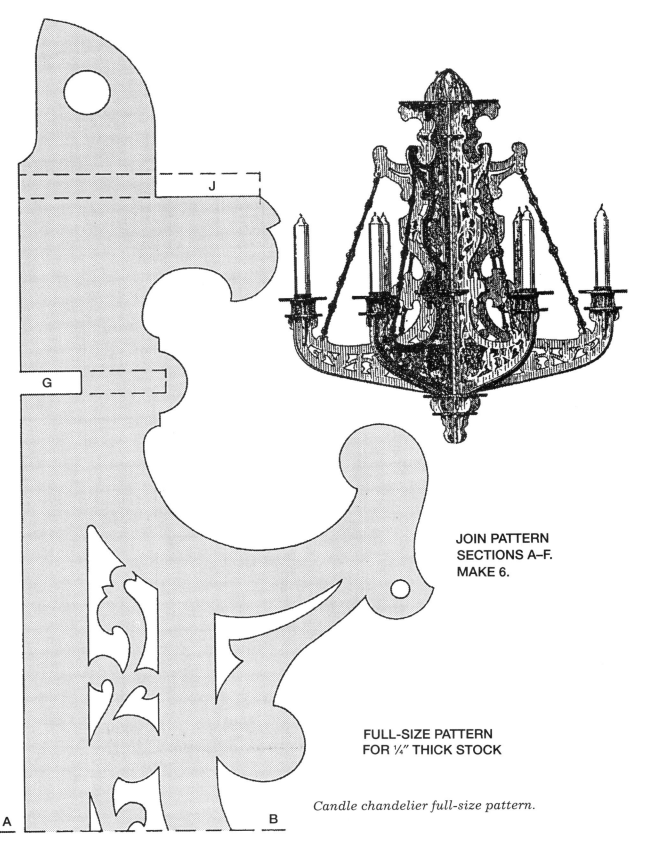

J

G

JOIN PATTERN SECTIONS A–F. MAKE 6.

FULL-SIZE PATTERN FOR ¼" THICK STOCK

Candle chandelier full-size pattern.

A   B

173

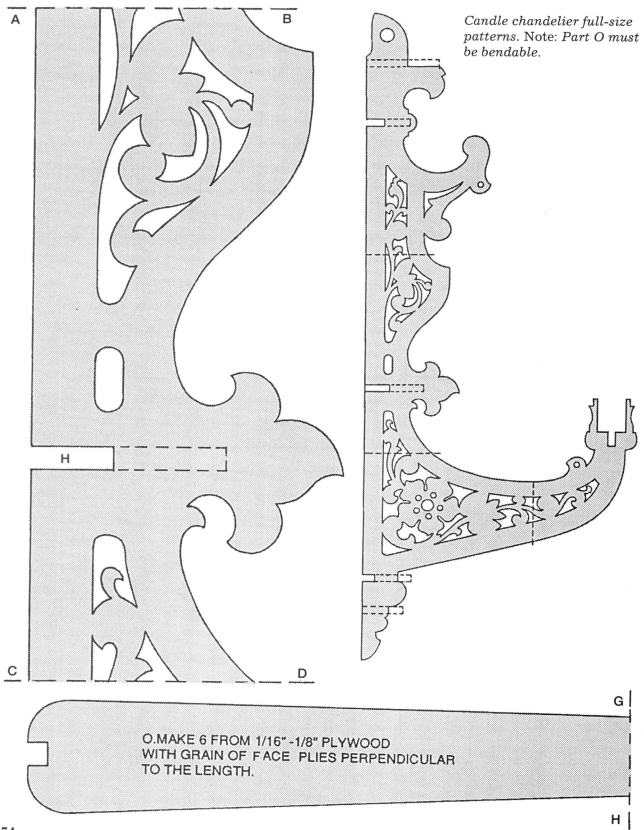

Candle chandelier full-size patterns. Note: Part O must be bendable.

A

B

H

C

D

O. MAKE 6 FROM 1/16"-1/8" PLYWOOD WITH GRAIN OF FACE PLIES PERPENDICULAR TO THE LENGTH.

G

H

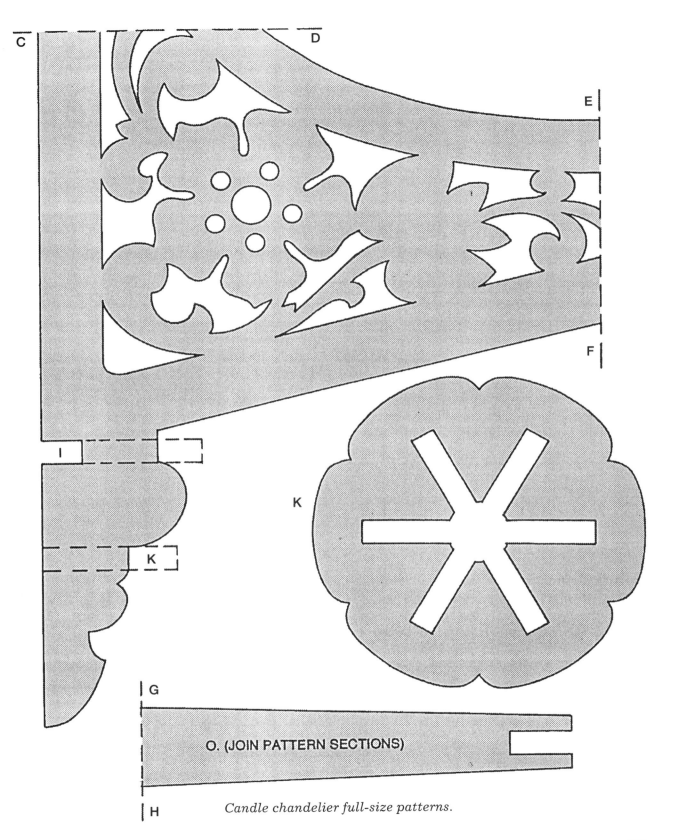

C

D

E

F

I

K

K

G

O. (JOIN PATTERN SECTIONS)

H

Candle chandelier full-size patterns.

175

Candle chandelier full-size patterns.

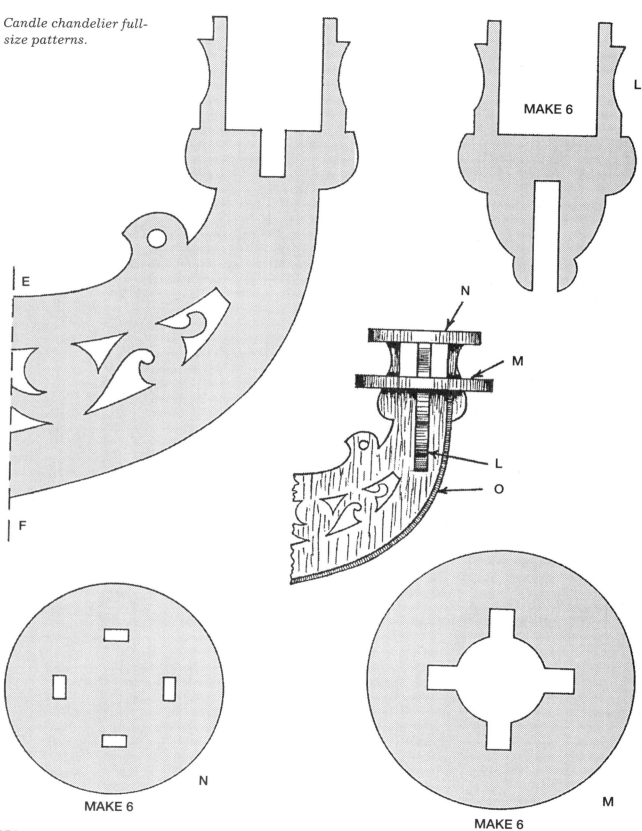

MAKE 6

L

E

F

N

M

L

O

MAKE 6

N

MAKE 6

M

Candle chandelier full-size patterns.

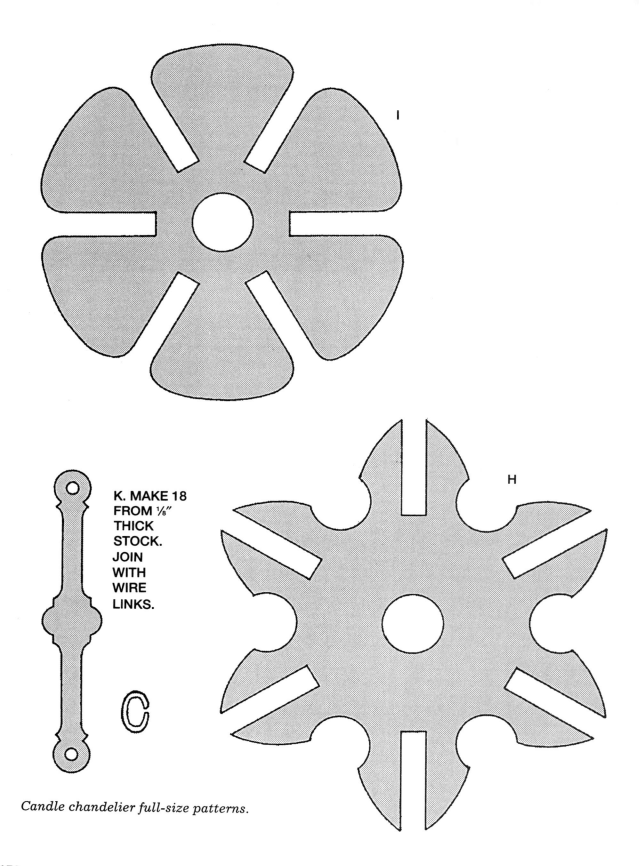

I

H

K. MAKE 18
FROM ⅛″
THICK
STOCK.
JOIN
WITH
WIRE
LINKS.

C

Candle chandelier full-size patterns.

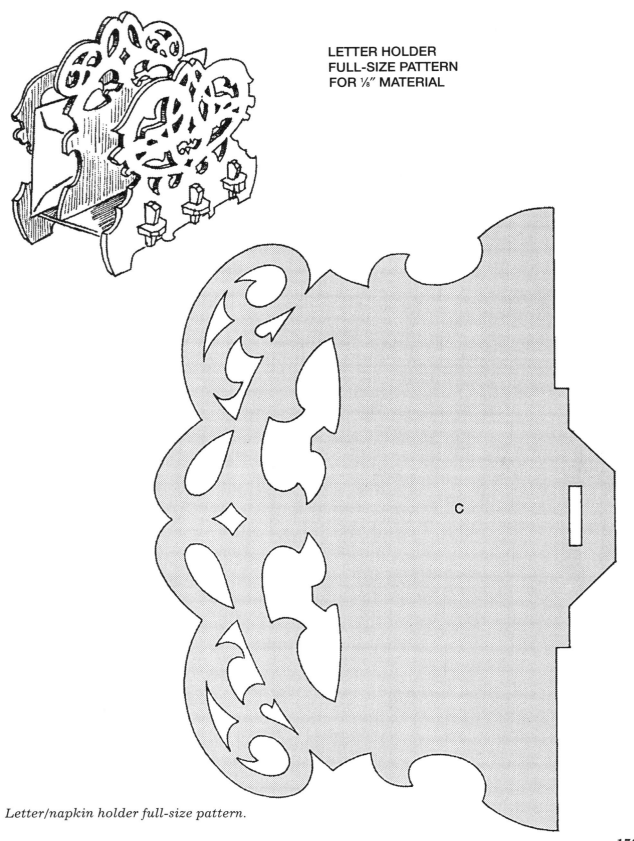

LETTER HOLDER
FULL-SIZE PATTERN
FOR ⅛″ MATERIAL

C

Letter/napkin holder full-size pattern.

179

LETTER HOLDER

A. MAKE 2. ➔

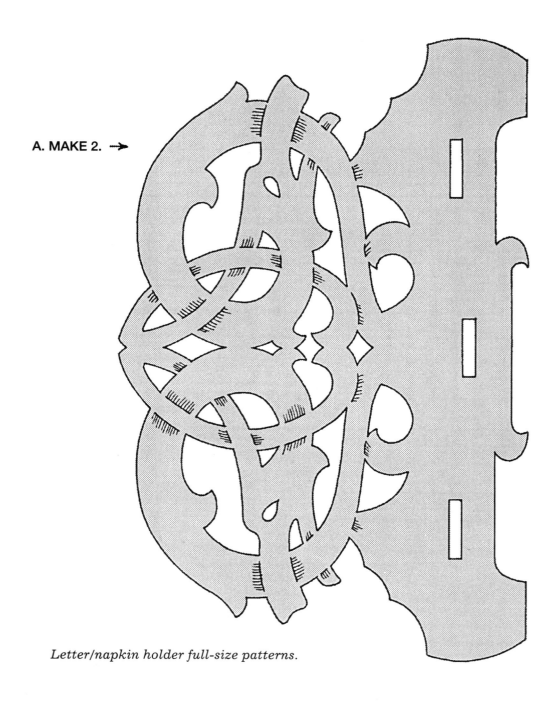

Letter/napkin holder full-size patterns.

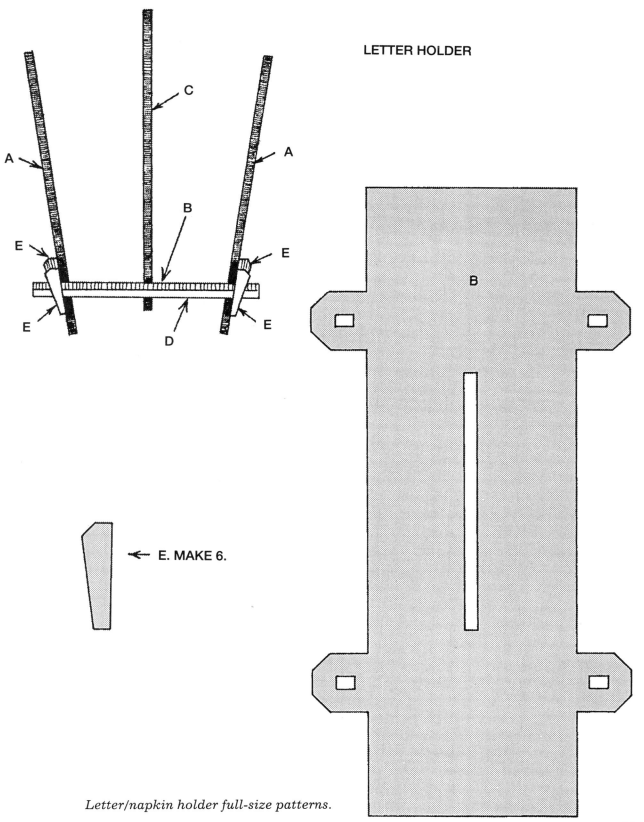

LETTER HOLDER

A

A

C

B

E

E

E

E

D

B

E. MAKE 6.

Letter/napkin holder full-size patterns.

181

Decorative stars created from six identical interlocking pieces.

Birds-in-a-tree cutout.

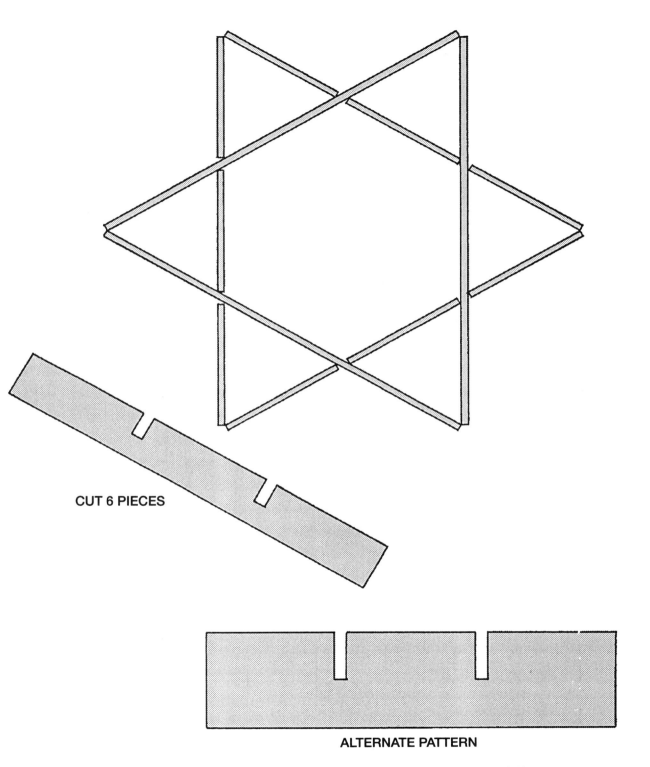

CUT 6 PIECES

ALTERNATE PATTERN

Decorative-star full-size patterns.

¼″ TO ½″
THICK

BASE,
⅜″ × 1¼″ × 3″

Full-size pattern for birds-in-a-tree cutout.

Current Books by Patrick Spielman

The Art of the Scroll Saw: Award Winning Designs

Wander through a spectacular, full-color gallery of extraordinary and imaginative scroll saw projects. Spielman is the tour guide through this exquisite exhibit of the work of 28 of the most widely known and productive woodworking artists in the United States and around the world. Follow their guidance and patterns and make an exciting assortment of 35 items, including doll furniture, a collapsible basket, a complete chess set, charming miniature clocks, a train puzzle, bookends, a picture frame, and much more. 160 full-color pages.

Carving Wild Animals: Life-Size Wood Figures

Spielman and renowned woodcarver Bill Dehos show how to carve more than 20 magnificent creatures of the North American wild. A cougar, black bear, prairie dog, squirrel, raccoon, and fox are some of the life-size animals included. Step-by-step, photo-filled instructions and multiple-view patterns, plus tips on the use of tools, wood selection, finishing, and polishing, help bring each animal to life. Oversized. Over 300 photos. 16 pages in full color. 240 pages.

Christmas Scroll Saw Patterns

Patrick and Patricia Spielman provide over 200 original, full-size scroll saw patterns with Christmas as the theme, including: toys, shelves, tree, window, and table decorations; segmented projects; and alphabets. A wide variety of Santas, trees, and holiday animals is included, as is a short, illustrated review of scroll saw techniques. 4 pages in color. 164 pages.

Classic Fretwork Scroll Saw Patterns

Spielman and coauthor James Reidle provide over 140 imaginative patterns inspired by and derived from mid- to late-19th-century scroll-saw masters. This book covers nearly 30 categories of patterns and includes a brief review of scroll-saw techniques and how to work with patterns. The patterns include ornamental numbers and letters, beautiful birds, signs, wall pockets, silhouettes, a sleigh, jewelry boxes, toy furniture, and more. 192 pages.

Country Mailboxes

Spielman and coauthor Paul Meisel have come up with the 20 best country-style mailbox designs. They include an old pump fire wagon, a Western saddle, a Dalmatian, and even a boy fishing. Simple instructions cover cutting, painting, decorating, and installation. Over 200 illustrations. 4 pages in color. 164 pages.

Gluing & Clamping

A thorough, up-to-date examination of one of the most critical steps in woodworking. Spielman explores the features of every type of glue—from traditional animal-hide glues to the newest epoxies—the clamps and tools needed, the bonding properties of different wood species, safety tips, and all techniques from edge-to-edge and end-to-end gluing to applying plastic laminates. Also included is a glossary of terms. Over 500 illustrations. 256 pages.

Making Country-Rustic Wood Projects

Hundreds of photos, patterns, and detailed scaled drawings reveal construction methods, woodworking techniques, and Spielman's professional secrets for making indoor and outdoor furniture in the distinctly attractive Country-Rustic style. Covered are all aspects of furniture making from choosing the best wood for the job to texturing smooth boards. Among the dozens of projects are mailboxes, cabinets, shelves, coffee tables, weather vanes, doors, panelling, plant stands, and many other durable and economical pieces. 400 illustrations. 4 pages in color. 164 pages.

Making Wood Bowls with a Router & Scroll Saw

Using scroll-saw rings, inlays, fretted edges, and much more, Spielman and master craftsman Carl Roehl have developed a completely new approach to creating decorative bowls. Over 200 illustrations. 8 pages in color. 168 pages.

Making Wood Decoys

This clear, step-by-step approach to the basics of decoy carving is abundantly illustrated with close-up photos for designing, selecting, and obtaining woods; tools; feather detailing; painting; and finishing of decorative and working decoys. Six different professional decoy artists are featured. Photo gallery (4 pages in full color) along with numerous detailed plans for various popular decoys. 164 pages.

Making Wood Signs

Designing, selecting woods and tools, and every process through finishing clearly covered. Instructions for hand- and power-carving, routing, and sandblasting techniques for small to huge signs. Foolproof guides for professional letters and ornaments. Hundreds of photos (4 pages in full color). Lists sources for supplies and special tooling. 148 pages.

New Router Handbook

This updated and expanded version of the definitive guide to routing continues to revolutionize router use. The text, with over 1,000 illustrations, covers familiar and new routers, bits, accessories, and tables available today; complete maintenance and safety techniques; a multitude of techniques for both hand-held and mounted routers; plus dozens of helpful shop-made fixtures and jigs. 384 pages.

Original Scroll Saw Shelf Patterns

Patrick Spielman and Loren Raty provide over 50 original, full-size patterns for wall shelves, which may be copied and applied directly to wood. Photographs of finished shelves are included, as well as information on choosing woods, stack sawing, and finishing. 4 pages in color. 132 pages.

Realistic Decoys

Spielman and master carver Keith Bridenhagen reveal their successful techniques for carving, feather texturing, painting, and finishing wood decoys. Details you can't find elsewhere—anatomy, attitudes, markings, and the easy, step-by-step approach to perfect delicate procedures—make this book invaluable. Includes listings for contests, shows, and sources of tools and supplies. 274 close-up photos. 8 pages in color. 232 pages.

Router Basics

With over 200 close-up, step-by-step photos and drawings, this valuable starter handbook will guide the new owner, as well as provide a spark to owners for whom the router isn't the tool they turn to most often. Covers all the basic router styles, along with how-it-works descriptions of all its major features. Includes sections on bits and accessories, as well as square-cutting and trimming, case and furniture routing, cutting circles and arcs, template and freehand routing, and using the router with a router table. 128 pages.

Router Jigs & Techniques

A practical encyclopedia of information, covering the latest equipment to use with the router, it describes all the newest commercial routing machines, along with jigs, bits, and other aids and devices. The book

not only provides invaluable tips on how to determine which router and bits to buy, it explains how to get the most out of the equipment once it is bought. Over 800 photos and illustrations. 384 pages.

Scroll Saw Basics

Features more than 275 illustrations covering basic techniques and accessories. Sections include types of saws, features, selection of blades, safety, and how to use patterns. Half a dozen patterns are included to help the scroll saw user get started. Basic cutting techniques are covered, including inside cuts, bevel cuts, stack-sawing, and others. 128 pages.

Scroll Saw Country Patterns

With 300 full-size patterns in 28 categories, this selection of projects covers an extraordinary range, with instructions every step of the way. Projects include farm animals, people, birds, and butterflies, plus letter and key holders, coasters, switch plates, country hearts, and more. Directions for piercing, drilling, sanding, and finishing, as well as tips on using special tools. 4 pages in color. 196 pages.

Scroll Saw Fretwork Patterns

This companion book to *Scroll Saw Fretwork Techniques & Projects* features over 200 fabulous, full-size fretwork patterns. These patterns, drawn by James Reidle, include popular classic designs, plus an array of imaginative contemporary ones. Choose from a variety of numbers, signs, brackets, animals, miniatures, and silhouettes, and more. 256 pages.

Scroll Saw Fretwork Techniques & Projects

A study in the historical development of

fretwork, as well as the tools, techniques, materials, and project styles that have evolved over the past 130 years. Every intricate turn and cut is explained, with over 550 step-by-step photos and illustrations. Patterns for all 32 projects are shown in full color. The book also covers some modern scroll-sawing machines as well as state-of-the-art fretwork and fine scroll-sawing techniques. 8 pages in color. 232 pages.

Scroll Saw Handbook

The workshop manual to this versatile tool includes the basics (how scroll saws work, blades to use, etc.) and the advantages and disadvantages of the general types and specific brand-name models on the market. All cutting techniques are detailed, including compound and bevel sawing, making inlays, reliefs, and recesses, cutting metals and other non-woods, and marquetry. There's even a section on transferring patterns to wood. Over 500 illustrations. 256 pages.

Scroll Saw Holiday Patterns

Patrick and Patricia Spielman provide over 100 full-size, shaded patterns for easy cutting, plus full-color photos of projects. Will serve all your holiday pleasures—all year long. Use these holiday patterns to create decorations, centerpieces, mailboxes, and diverse projects to keep or give as gifts. Standard holidays, as well as the four seasons, birthdays, and anniversaries, are represented. 8 pages of color. 168 pages.

Scroll Saw Pattern Book

The original classic pattern book—over 450 patterns for wall plaques, refrigerator magnets, candle holders, pegboards, jewelry, ornaments, shelves, brackets, picture frames, signboards, and many other proj-

ects. Beginning and experienced scroll saw users alike will find something to intrigue and challenge them. 256 pages.

Scroll Saw Patterns for the Country Home

Patrick and Patricia Spielman and Sherri Spielman Valitchka produce a wide-ranging collection of over 200 patterns on country themes, including simple cutouts, mobiles, shelves, sculpture, pull toys, door and window toppers, clock holders, photo frames, layered pictures, and more. Over 80 black-and-white photos and 8 pages of color photos help you to visualize the steps involved as well as the finished projects. General instructions in Spielman's clear and concise style are included. 200 pages.

Scroll Saw Puzzle Patterns

80 full-size patterns for jigsaw puzzles, stand-up puzzles, and inlay puzzles. With meticulous attention to detail, Patrick and Patricia Spielman provide instructions and step-by-step photos, along with tips on tools and wood selection, for making dinosaurs, camels, hippopotami, alligators—even a family of elephants! Inlay puzzle patterns include basic shapes, numbers, an accurate piece-together map of the United States, and a host of other colorful educational and enjoyable games for children. 8 pages of color. 264 pages.

Scroll Saw Shelf Patterns

Spielman and master scroll saw designer Loren Raty offer full-size patterns for 44 different shelf styles. Designs include wall shelves, corner shelves, and multi-tiered shelves. The patterns work well with 1/4-inch hardwood, plywood or any solid wood. Over 150 illustrations. 4 pages in color. 132 pages.

Scroll Saw Silhouette Patterns

With over 120 designs, Spielman and James Reidle provide an extremely diverse collection of intricate silhouette patterns, ranging from Victorian themes to sports to cowboys. They also include mammals, birds, country and nautical designs, as well as dragons, cars, and Christmas themes. Tips, hints, and advice are included along with detailed photos of finished works. 160 pages.

Sharpening Basics

The ultimate handbook that goes well beyond the "basics" to become the major up-to-date reference work features more than 300 detailed illustrations (mostly photos) explaining every facet of tool sharpening. Sections include bench-sharpening tools, sharpening machines, and safety. Chapters cover cleaning tools, and sharpening all sorts of tools, including chisels, plane blades (irons), hand knives, carving tools, turning tools, drill and boring tools, router and shaper tools, jointer and planer knives, drivers and scrapers, and, of course, saws. 128 pages.

Southwest Scroll Saw Patterns

Spielman and scroll-sawing wizard Dan Kihl present over 200 patterns inspired by the early cultures of the American Southwest. Designs include coyotes, buffalo, horses, lizards, snakes, pottery, cacti, cowboys, kokopelli figures and more. Incorporate them into all kinds of projects, key racks, clocks, signs, shelves, napkin holders, jewelry boxes, and more. Follow the suggestions for using copper inlay on projects, either for a bright, shiny look or chemically aged to a beautiful bluish green for striking results that are not commonly seen in scroll-saw work. 8 pages of color. 168 pages.

Spielman's Original Scroll Saw Patterns

262 full-size patterns that don't appear elsewhere feature teddy bears, dinosaurs, sports figures, dancers, cowboy cutouts, Christmas ornaments, and dozens more. Fretwork patterns are included for a Viking ship, framed cutouts, wall-hangers, keychain miniatures, jewelry, and much more. Hundreds of step-by-step photos and drawings show how to turn, repeat, and crop each design for thousands of variations. 4 pages of color. 228 pages.

Victorian Gingerbread: Patterns & Techniques

Authentic pattern designs (many full-size) cover the full range of indoor and outdoor detailing: brackets, corbels, shelves, grilles, spandrels, balusters, running trim, headers, valances, gable ornaments, screen doors, pickets, trellises, and much more. Also included are complete plans for Victorian mailboxes, house numbers, signs, and more. With clear instructions and helpful drawings by James Reidle, the book also provides tips for making gingerbread trim. 8 pages in color. 200 pages.

Victorian Scroll Saw Patterns

Intricate original designs plus classics from the 19th century are presented in full-size, shaded patterns. Instructions are provided with drawings and photos. Projects include alphabets and numbers, silhouettes and designs for shelves, frames, filigree baskets, plant holders, decorative boxes, picture frames, welcome signs, architectural ornaments, and much more. 160 pages.

Woodworker's Pattern Library: Alphabets & Designs

Spielman and daughter Sherri Spielman

Valitchka have come up with a collection of 40 alphabets and matching number patterns in the new series the *Woodworker's Pattern Library*. Upper- and lowercase alphabets are presented for all woodworking uses, including block script, italic, and a section on decorative design elements to complement uses of lettering. An introductory section on Basic Tips provides information on enlarging and transferring patterns as well as on making templates. 128 pages.

Woodworker's Pattern Library: Borders, Trim & Frames

Spielman and designer Brian Dahlen continue the popular series with a collection of dozens of decorative patterns for scroll saw enthusiasts. Styles range from the basic with simple lines and little detail, to ornate swirls and curls and pictorial motifs. Create unusual name plates, house numbers, or clocks. Frame works of art, bulletin boards, and anything else that calls out for some pizzazz. Repetitive linear designs are included, and will work especially well in architectural applications around doors, windows, and archways. Some can be used as furniture and cabinet overlays. 128 pages.

Woodworker's Pattern Library: Sports Figures

Spielman and Brian Dahlen have put together a full range of sports-related patterns for the new series the *Woodworker's Pattern Library*. Sports images for scroll-sawing enthusiasts include over 125 patterns in 34 categories of sporting activity. The patterns can be incorporated in functional projects such as signs or furniture and shelves or they can be used simply for decorative accent such as silhouettes in windows or against walls. An introductory section on Basic Tips provides information on enlarging and transferring patterns as well as on cutting techniques such as stack sawing. 128 pages.

Working Green Wood with PEG

Covers every process for making beautiful, inexpensive projects from green wood without cracking, splitting, or warping it. Hundreds of clear photos and drawings show every step from obtaining the raw wood through shaping, treating, and finishing PEG-treated projects. 175 unusual project ideas. Lists supply sources. 120 pages.

About the Authors

Patrick Spielman lives surrounded by a natural forest in the famous tourist area of Door County, in northeast Wisconsin. A graduate of the University of Wisconsin, Stout, he taught high school and vocational woodworking in Wisconsin public schools for 27 years. Patrick's love for wood and woodworking began between the ages of 8 and 10, when he transformed wooden fruit crates into toys. Encouragement from his parents, two older brothers, and a sister, who provided the basic tools to keep the youngster occupied, enabled Patrick to become a very productive woodworker at an early age. Today, he and his wife, Patricia, own Spielman's Wood Works and Spielman's Kid Works. Both are gift galleries that offer high-quality hand- and machine-crafted wood products produced locally and in other countries around the world. Patrick left the school classroom in 1985, but he continues to teach and share his designs and ideas through his published works. He has written over 50 woodworking books, some of which have been translated into Dutch and German. In 1994 he won the National Association of Home and Workshop Writers' best how-to book award for his updated book on routers, *The New Router Handbook.*

Gösta Dahlqvist was born in 1918 in a small town in Sweden. His father was a craftsman who made clogs, and Gösta worked in the same factory as a young boy. In the 1930s, Gösta started experimenting with figure sawing and it became a lifelong hobby. He used a common, simple bow saw, cutting patterns shown in a weekly magazine, the *Allers Familie Journal.*

Gösta worked in the engineering industry for almost 40 years and it wasn't until his retirement at age 60 that he really concentrated on his sawing. His interest in figure sawing increased when he sent away for several books by Patrick Spielman. "My own creativity increases when I see and read about others' ideas. I have made a lot of friends through my sawing," he says.

Should you wish to write Pat or Gösta, please forward your letters to Sterling Publishing Company.

CHARLES NURNBERG
STERLING PUBLISHING COMPANY

Index

Pages in bold are in color section